A Scrapbook of Quilts

Joanna Figueroa   Carrie Nelson

Carrie and Joanna have been "quilting friends" for over a decade and have each admired the other's work from afar. Joanna's scrappy style is almost always "Fig Tree" based with a few other favorites thrown in for extra measure. She also loves mixing solids with a multitude of small cream prints, as well as creating more limited seasonal palettes that are still super scrappy. She says that her greatest motivation in working on a book is that she gets to do "what she wants" and is not constrained by a single fabric collection! Carrie has always been the queen of scrappy ... and along with our good friend, Lissa Alexander, is known for her scrappy genius in the quilting community! She loves to incorporate some Fig Tree fabric but uses dozens of other collections in any given project and can still make it look fabulous. That is certainly a skill!

When the idea of writing a book together was presented, they both jumped at the chance and have never looked back! Once they chose their six blocks, three favorites each, they planned and designed each of their versions and the journey began. To add to the scrappiness of the project, they decided to invite six special quilting colleagues to help them interpret each block. Those friends are Susan Ache, Melissa Corry, Anna Dineen, Kimberly Jolly, Chelsi Stratton and Susan Vaughan. You can read a little about these ladies in each chapter alongside their project.

As the projects developed, both Carrie and Joanna asked several of their closest quilt friends to join them in working on each of their versions. Those friends include: Judy Adams, Cynthia Bird, Thelma Childers, Megan Edgerton, Cheryl Hadley, Carrie Straka and Susan Vaughan. "It takes a village" is for sure the way this book got done, and Joanna and Carrie couldn't be more grateful for each person that jumped in to help!! Last but certainly not least, Joanna and Carrie invited their favorite quilters to put their magical touch on so many of these projects. Thank you Marion Bott, Maggie Honeyman, Diana Johnson, Teresa Silva and Carrie Straka.

And now Joanna and Carrie invite you, their quilting friends everywhere, to work your way through this book full of scrappy goodness ... and choose your next favorite project. They hope you find lots of inspiration and ideas and that this becomes one of those books with torn and tattered corners and marks in the margins. A well loved book that you can use again and again.

"Wishing you a wonderful quilting journey!"

Joanna & Carrie

Joanna Figueroa

Carrie Nelson

Instagram: @figtreeandco
Blog: blog.figtreeandcompany.com

Instagram: @justcarrieintexas

Table of Contents

The Process with Joanna and Carrie

It's All About Color

« Joanna »

I know that the process of design is very individual, and every artist begins in a different place. For me, it has always been about color. From the first early paintings that I pinned to clotheslines and sold to the neighbors, to my latest fabric collection, my quilting and design journey has always been about color first. The colors that I am drawn to, time and time again, are those from a "vintage palette" ... they literally make my heart skip a beat. If you look at old children's book drawings or fruit crate labels or travel illustrations from the early 1900s, you'll notice that they often chose colors that were just a little bit "off" as we would say today—not the color combination that you might expect to see. I love to try to capture that vintage feel when I am designing. I love to refer to these colors and palettes as "forgotten" colors, because there is just something about them that feels like I'm traveling back to another time.

To create that palette, whether it be for a fabric collection or for an individual project, I definitely have a "go to" palette that I am drawn to and then make individual "color stories" based on what I am trying to communicate. But my favorite colors are always those that have a warm and vintage feeling, even if they are sometimes bright and more modern in combination! Reds are more tomato reds, orangey and soft. Greens are more limey or chartreuse. Blues are more aqua, with slightly green overtones. Pinks are more likely to be peach and apricot. Even blacks and greys can be warm or cool. If you started laying black fabrics next to each other you'd be amazed to see the amount of difference there is between a warmer and a cooler black.

« Carrie »

For me, it's more about the source of inspiration. It can be a color palette, a block, a collection or even a single piece of fabric. Sometimes it's simply the challenge of "Can I make something with that?"

When I think about color, what keeps coming through is how personal the choices are. We can use different terminology, and the process can be different, but in the end, there are things we do because color speaks to us in some way.

I like experimenting so there aren't too many palettes that I haven't played with at some point. Some have definitely worked better than others, and the truth is that I've learned more from the failures than the successes.

"Color is a power which directly influences the soul."

Wassily Kandinsky

New Neutrals

« Joanna »

Another principle that I often work with is that yellow goes with everything! There is no color on the color wheel that looks bad with yellow. Think about it. Many of the most classic color combinations are paired with yellow, yet somehow people seem to be afraid of yellow! I really don't know why that is. Of course, the yellows I like are a soft butter yellow, warm mustard yellow or strong cream yellow. These yellows often form a key element of the color palettes I work with. The strength of the yellow depends on what feeling I am trying to convey or what color combination I am trying to create.

« Carrie »

Red is a neutral. It goes with everything. While I don't use much yellow, it is always a good addition to a scrap quilt. (Just like red.) I think it really comes down to using colors that you love and finding the shade and hue that works with the rest of the palette.

Figuring Out What You Like

« Carrie »

When you see a quilt you absolutely love, do you ever ask yourself what is it that caught your attention? Is it the color palette? Is it the kind of fabrics used? So much of what Joanna shares about "Instant Vintage" are details that go unnoticed unless we really look at quilts we love. It also means really looking at quilts we've made that didn't quite work.

I love using large florals and big-scale prints for small pieces, including backgrounds. I love the "moosh" factor they get. In addition to getting different fabric combinations, the prints don't have the high contrast, or hard edges, that small-scale prints have in piecing. It's the same with using fabric combinations that are high-contrast and some that are lower-contrast.

The Process with Joanna and Carrie

Instant Vintage

« Joanna »

A couple of things that I always try to add to any project if possible are:

- Dots: small, medium or large, it doesn't matter! Dots add a retro, classic feel to any project.

- Something geometric: little stripes or tiny geometrics. They add a bit of instant vintage every time

- Large florals: Every time you cut up a large floral print, you get a dozen different fabric combos depending on which part of the floral you have cut up. It adds "instant sparkle" to your blocks, and no two pieces ever look the same.

« Carrie »

What she said. I also like using different amounts of fabrics and using some in only one or two places. Most old quilts were made with scraps. Literally. There were bits of some fabrics and more of others. If there's one drawback of using precuts, it's that the fabrics tend to be evenly used. So if the cutting calls for a Layer Cake, I'll add some cut pieces from a charm pack of a different collection.

Grounding Colors

« Joanna »

I always try to add some colors to "ground" my quilts. Many quilters stay within the medium range of tones, never branching out into true lights or true darks. I've heard this over and over again in classes and workshops throughout my career. Personally, I've never struggled with adding cream and ivory as my lights but adding darks has been another story altogether. Because they are not my favorite colors, I have needed to learn how to add them successfully. Learning how to add good dark browns, warm blacks, deep plums and soft greys has added a strong grounding element to my designs. These colors give your eye somewhere to rest as it moves around the myriad of other colors in your project. They help to give your overall project a more vintage, aged feel and round out your color palette which strengthens the other color choices you have made. You will be amazed at what a few well placed taupes or browns can add to an otherwise medium toned quilt!

« Carrie »

I think of grounding colors as a range – making sure that the values being used aren't always in the middle, the mediums. While this is something I've always done, it took me a while to understand what it meant and the difference it made. I just knew that was what I liked.

To me, this means having a range of values in the lights, especially if they're used as a background for blocks. For a quilt like Pirouette, my color palette is yellow, red and blue. Using prints that are almost 50/50 white and red, or those that are almost entirely red with just a tiny bit of white or other color gives a wide range of value within a single color. The blues range from light blue to navy.

Even with a palette that is lighter or darker overall, I include fabrics that expand the color range.

The Process with Joanna and Carrie

The Infamous 80/20 Principle

« Joanna »

I know Carrie likes to joke with me a little bit about this one, but I sincerely think it's because she agrees with me! Right, Carrie? One of the questions I get the most often is, "How do you start a quilt, especially a scrappy quilt and make it your own?" So while teaching, I came up with the 80/20 Principle and it goes something like this … choose a favorite fabric collection – one that you love. Study it and see what you could add to it that would make it pop, would make it your own or would just make it a little bit different. Add 20% of those "other" things that aren't in there to begin with. Maybe it's a color that you think is missing or is your favorite, maybe it's a few large scale prints to cut up, maybe you even want to take something out that isn't your favorite. You would be surprised how much a collection can change simply by taking out one color and replacing it with something else. So keep about 80% of the collection that you fell in love with because you did fall in love with it for a reason. Then add 20% of something that makes it different and makes it "you". If you are confident in your scrappy choices, you can just keep going from there, but this is definitely a great starting point.

« Carrie »

I do agree with this! And I do like to tease Joanna about having a rule that she named. Even if the exact proportion isn't 80/20, the goal is to change it up, to make it more "you". Even if it means adding more of the pieces within the collection you fell in love with, you've changed the balance and given it your own spin.

As I think about what we've both said, so much of what we both do is "making it our own". Oregon Trail is a good example of that. This started with a bundle Joanna put together using fabrics from three different Moda fabric designers. I loved the colors and the mix of fabrics. And it was perfect for this pattern. I added a few pieces for more variety because … why not? As the quilt started coming together, it needed more blocks because I loved how it looked without borders. I think it changes the balance of the quilt by putting a greater focus on the blocks.

That's my variation of the 80/20 rule. I follow 80% of the pattern.

Use ¼" seams and press as arrows indicate throughout.
WOF = width of fabric

Joanna's Top 5 Notions

1. **Vintage Strawberry Mini Cutting Mat**
   (SKU# ISE-741) My sweet double-sided cutting mat will make cutting a breeze and spruce up your sewing room! The measurement markings go up to 5" x 7" and the self-healing mat is strong and durable.

2. **Little House Glass Head Pins**
   (SKU# 1052) are my favorite, but **Clover Fine Quilting Pins** (SKU #2509) are a close second.

3. **6" Medium Perfect Applique Scissors**
   (SKU# KKBPSM) by Karen Kay Buckley

4. **6" x 12" Ruler** (SKU# OG12) by Omnigrid

5. **Tuscany Collection Cotton Batting** by Hobbs

Carrie's Top 5 Notions

1. **Little House Glass Head Pins** (SKU# 1052) are my favorite too, and I might have stashed a box or two! **Dritz Ultra-Fine Glass Head Pins** (SKU# 172) are next on the list.

2. **Olfa Frosted Acrylic Non-slip Rulers.** I love all of them. The 4 ½" square (SKU# 1071797) and 6" x 12" (SKU# 1071819) are my most used.

3. **Clover White Seam Ripper** (SKU# 482) For those very, very rare occasions when I must un-sew a seam. I love these because the point is fine, and the little cutter in the curve is very sharp.

4. **50wt Aurifil Stone 100% Cotton Mako Cone Thread** (SKU# MK50CO-2324) Best. Buy. Ever. (And a pretty cone holder, of course.)

5. **Omnigrid 4" Needlecraft Scissors** (SKU# OG2064) Super-sharp small scissors for clipping threads, seams and trimming at the machine.

How to Finish a Pincushion

Fabric Requirements:

Scraps - Backing

Cut slightly larger than the Pincushion Top

Scraps - Cotton Batting (the thinner, the better)

Cut two pieces slightly larger than the Pincushion Top

Filling or Stuffing

Carrie likes to use crushed walnut shells for filling, but you can use aquarium sand.

She also likes to use 100% cotton stuffing or scrap batting right at the end to prevent spillage.

Optional

A funnel and scoop are helpful to fill the pincushions, and using a small pan with a lip helps catch the spillage.

Carrie recommends using 80wt Aurifil 100% cotton thread for quilting.

Quilted Pincushion Top:

With right sides up, layer the Pincushion Top with one piece of Batting.

Quilt as desired. Trim excess Batting.

Baste ⅛" around the inside of the Quilted Pincushion Top.

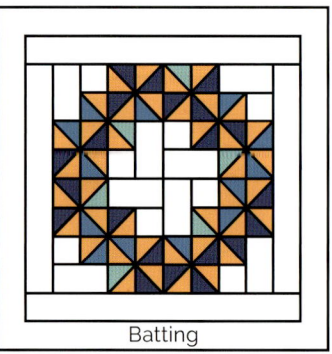

Batting

Quilted Pincushion Back:

With right sides up, layer the Backing fabric with one piece of Batting.

Quilt as desired. Trim to the same size as the Quilted Pincushion Top.

Baste ⅛" around the inside of the Quilted Pincushion Back.

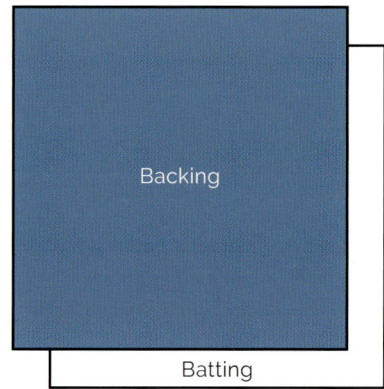

Backing

Batting

Finishing:

With right sides facing, layer the Quilted Pincushion Top with the Quilted Pincushion Back. Pin in place.

Sew ¼" around the edges, leaving a small section open.

Turn right side out and add filling.

Whip stitch or tack stitch the opening closed with matching thread.

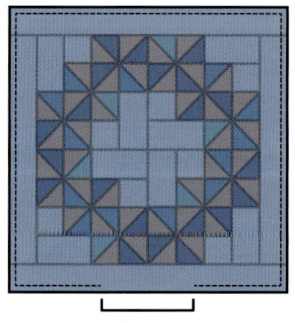

Small opening

How to Finish a Pillow

Fabric Requirements:

	14" x 26" Pillow	16" x 20" Pillow	20" square Pillow	25" square Pillow
Optional Binding	⅓ yard 3 - 2 ¼" x WOF strips	⅓ yard 3 - 2 ¼" x WOF strips	⅓ yard 3 - 2 ¼" x WOF strips	⅓ yard 3 - 2 ¼" x WOF strips
Backing	1 yard 2 - 15 ½" x 31 ½" rectangles	1 ⅛ yards 2 - 17 ½" x 25 ½" rectangles	1 ⅓ yards 2 - 21 ½" x 25 ½" rectangles	1 ⅝ yards 2 - 26 ½" x 31 ½" rectangles
Batting	Craft Size 1 - 15 ½" x 27 ½" rectangle	Craft Size 1 - 17 ½" x 21 ½" rectangle	Craft Size 1 - 21 ½" square	Craft Size 1 - 26 ½" square
Muslin	⅝ yard 1 - 15 ½" x 27 ½" rectangle	⅝ yard 1 - 17 ½" x 21 ½" rectangle	¾ yard 1 - 21 ½" square	⅞ yard 1 - 26 ½" square
Pillow Form	14" x 26" pillow	16" x 20" pillow	20" square pillow	24" square pillow or 26" square pillow

Quilted Pillow Top:

Layer the Pillow Top, the Batting and the Muslin. Quilt as desired. Trim excess Batting and Muslin. Baste ⅛" around the inside of the Quilted Pillow Top. Quilted Pillow Top will shrink after quilting.

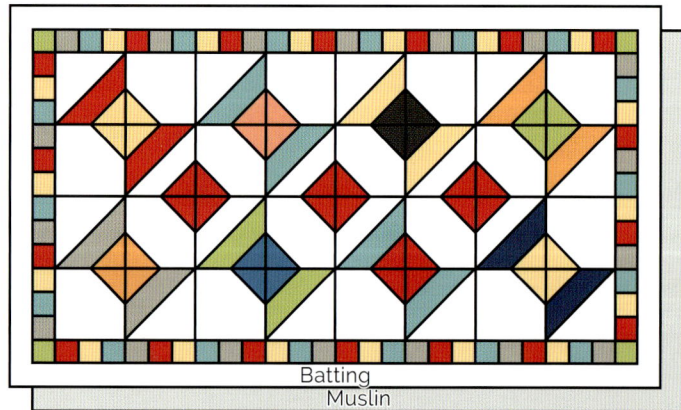

Batting
Muslin

Pillow Back:

With wrong sides facing, fold each Backing rectangle in half.

Partial Pillow Back should measure:

14" x 26" Pillow	16" x 20" Pillow	20" square Pillow	25" square Pillow
15 ½" x 15 ¾" rectangle	12 ¾" x 17 ½" rectangle	12 ¾" x 21 ½" rectangle	15 ¾" x 26 ½" rectangle

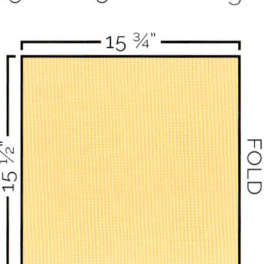 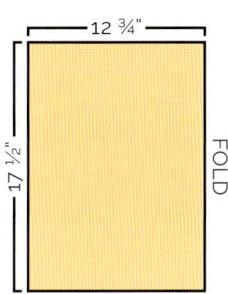 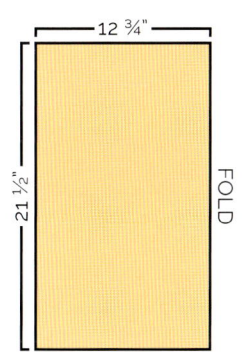 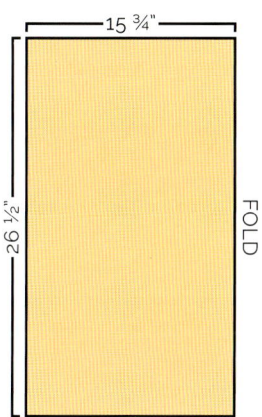

Layer two Partial Pillow Backs and overlap them with folds in the center and raw edges on the outside. Pin in place.

Pillow Back should measure:

14" x 26" Pillow	16" x 20" Pillow	20" square Pillow	25" square Pillow
15 ½" x 27 ½" rectangle	17 ½" x 21 ½" rectangle	21 ½" square	26 ½" square

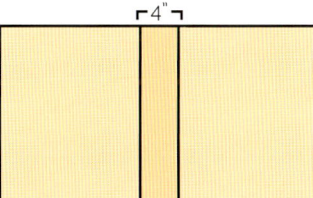 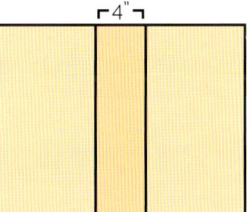 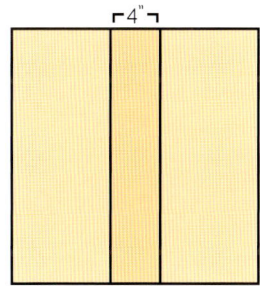 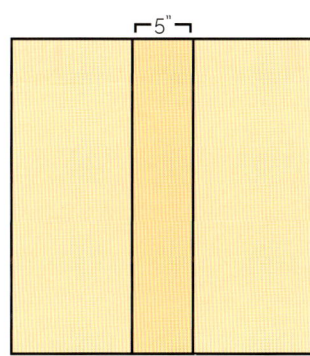

Finishing with Binding:

Layer the Quilted Pillow Top right side up on the Pillow Back.

TRIM Pillow Back to the size of the Quilted Pillow Top.

Baste ⅛" around the edges.

Piece the binding strips end to end for binding.

Bind as desired.

Finishing without Binding:

With right sides together, layer the Quilted Pillow Top with the Pillow Back.

TRIM Pillow Back to the size of the Quilted Pillow Top.

Using a ¼" seam allowance, stitch around the edges.

Turn the pillow right sides out.

Chapter 1:
Vintage Spools

by Joanna Figueroa

"There is something about spool quilt blocks that immediately takes me back to a simpler time. I sit down at my sewing machine and imagine hand sewing, the old black and gold Singer Featherweights purring along and a quilt bee with a dozen quilting friends gathered to sew. For this project, I wanted to combine two different kinds of spool blocks, as well as the whole rainbow of my favorite Fig Tree fabrics for a totally scrappy quilt. Since it was stitched and quilted during 2020, it will always remind me of a crazy year when everything was turned upside down, and yet we all quilted our way through it! I can't wait to throw this one in the wash and 'crinkle' it all up for even more of a vintage feel."

Joanna

"I don't know what Joanna's thread box looks like, but mine is a bit of a jumble with a crazy mix of spools in different colors, weights and sizes. So mixing two spool blocks is one of my favorite things about this quilt.

As it was for Joanna, this quilt reflects 2020 with unexpected changes in direction, embracing bumps in the road and finding joy in the moment. That's why my quilt has some piecing in the middle of the spool and a random mix of blocks."

Carrie

Side
Vintage Spools
Block

6 ½" x 6 ½" unfinished

Cutting Instructions:

Description		Cutting
Background	A	1 - 4" square
	B	2 - 3 ½" squares
Inner Spool	C	4 - 2" squares
Outer Spool	D	1 - 4" square

Piecing Instructions:

Draw a diagonal line on the wrong side of the Fabric A square.

With right sides facing, layer the Fabric A square with the Fabric D square.

Stitch ¼" from each side of the drawn line.

Cut apart on the marked line.

TRIM Half Square Triangle Unit to measure 3 ½" x 3 ½".

Make two.

Draw a diagonal line on the wrong side of the Fabric C squares.

With right sides facing, layer a Fabric C square on the bottom left corner of a Half Square Triangle Unit.

Stitch on the drawn line and trim ¼" away from the seam.

Outer Spool Unit should measure 3 ½" x 3 ½".

Make two.

With right sides facing, layer a Fabric C square on the bottom right corner of a Fabric B square.

Stitch on the drawn line and trim ¼" away from the seam.

Inner Spool Unit should measure 3 ½" x 3 ½".

Make two.

Assemble Block. Press open.

Side Vintage Spools Block should measure 6 ½" x 6 ½".

Make one.

Straight Vintage Spools Block

6 ½" x 6 ½" unfinished

Cutting Instructions:

Description		Cutting
Background	A	2 - 1 ⅝" x 3 ½" rectangles
	B	4 - 1 ⅝" squares
	C	2 - 1" x 6 ½" rectangles
Inner Spool	D	1 - 3 ½" square
Outer Spool	E	2 - 2" x 5 ¾" rectangles

Piecing Instructions:

Draw a diagonal line on the wrong side of the Fabric B squares.

With right sides facing, layer a Fabric B square on the bottom left corner of a Fabric E rectangle.

Stitch on the drawn line and trim ¼" away from the seam.

Repeat on the bottom right corner.

Outer Spool Unit should measure 2" x 5 ¾".

Make two.

Assemble Unit.

Inner Spool Unit should measure 3 ½" x 5 ¾".

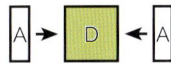 

Make one.

Assemble Unit.

Straight Vintage Spools Unit should measure 5 ¾" x 6 ½".

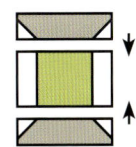 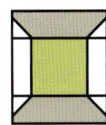

Make one.

Assemble Block.

TRIM Straight Vintage Spools Block to measure 6 ½" x 6 ½".

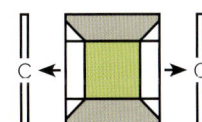 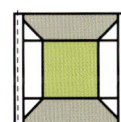 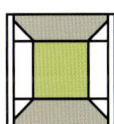

Make one.

Joanna's Vintage Spools Quilt

68 ½" x 68 ½"

Designed by: Joanna Figueroa / Sewn by: Joanna Figueroa and Cheryl Hadley
Quilted by: Marion Bott (Instagram: @bottmarion)

Fabric Requirements:

22 Print Fat Eighths* - Blocks	
From each 9" x 21" rectangle cut:	
2 - 4" squares (44 total)	A
2 - 3 ½" squares (44 total)	B
4 - 2" x 5 ¾" rectangles (88 total)	C
8 - 2" squares (176 total)	D

22 Low Volume Fat Eighths** - Side Vintage Spools Block Background and Middle Border	
From each 9" x 21" rectangle cut:	
2 - 4" squares (44 total)	E
4 - 4" squares (88 total)	F
4 - 3 ½" squares (88 total)	G

1 ⅓ yards - Straight Vintage Spools Block Background	
17 - 1 ⅝" x WOF strips, subcut into:	
88 - 1 ⅝" x 3 ½" rectangles	H
176 - 1 ⅝" squares	I
15 - 1" x WOF strips, subcut into:	
88 - 1" x 6 ½" rectangles	J

⅜ yard - Inner Border	
6 - 1 ½" x WOF strips, sew end to end and subcut into:	
2 - 1 ½" x 54 ½" strips	K1
2 - 1 ½" x 56 ½" strips	K2

1 ¼ yards - Middle Border	
16 - 2 ¼" x WOF strips, subcut into:	
272 - 2 ¼" squares	L

⅞ yard - Outer Border	
8 - 3" x WOF strips, sew end to end and subcut into:	
2 - 3" x 63 ½" strips	M1
2 - 3" x 68 ½" strips	M2

⅔ yard - Binding	
8 - 2 ¼" x WOF strips	N

4 ⅜ yards - Backing	

* Print Fat Eighth cutting:

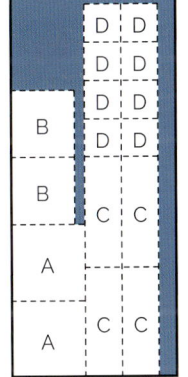

** Low Volume Fat Eighth cutting:

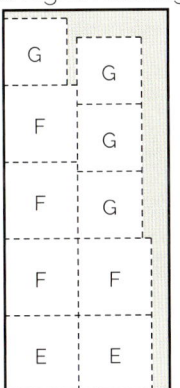

Joanna's Vintage Spools Quilt

Off the Cuff ...
PINNING

« Carrie »

True confessions. I don't pin all that much. I know when I need to and the rest of the time I don't pin any more than I have to. And yes, I have been known to sew over pins.

« Joanna »

I'm pretty much right there with Carrie on this one. I don't love to pin. I will avoid it when I can. And I have sewn over a pin on many an occasion ... I will definitely slow down, but I do keep sewing! I know some of you will let me know how bad that is for me, my pins and my machine ... and I know, I know, but I can't help myself! I will definitely pin when I am really worried about two seams coming together, and I will pin quadrants when adding borders. Other than that, it's kind of a gamble my friends! If I can hold it together with my fingers and make it go where I want it to go, that is what I do most days.

Refer to page 18 for Side Vintage Spools Block instructions.

Side Vintage Spools Blocks:

Assemble Block using coordinating fabric. Side Vintage Spools Block should measure 6 ½" x 6 ½".

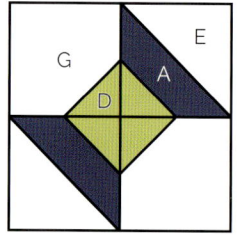

Make forty-four total.

Refer to page 19 for Straight Vintage Spools Block instructions.

Straight Vintage Spools Blocks:

Assemble Block using coordinating fabric. Straight Vintage Spools Block should measure 6 ½" x 6 ½".

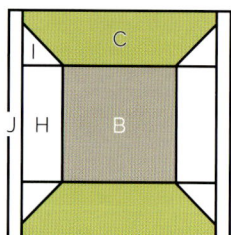

Make forty-four total.

Save your leftover blocks to make a pillow or sewing machine cover!

Quilt Center:

Assemble Quilt Center. Press toward Straight Vintage Spools Blocks.
Quilt Center should measure 54 ½" x 54 ½".

Joanna's Vintage Spools Quilt

Border:

Draw a diagonal line on the wrong side of the Fabric L squares.

With right sides facing, layer Fabric L squares on opposite corners of a Fabric F square.

Stitch on the drawn lines and trim ¼" away from the seams.

Repeat on the remaining corners.

Square in a Square Unit should measure 4" x 4".

Make sixty-eight total.

You will not use all Fabric F squares.

- -

Assemble Border using sixteen Square in a Square Units.

Side Middle Border should measure 4" x 56 ½".

Make two.

- -

Assemble Border using eighteen Square in a Square Units.

Top and Bottom Middle Border should measure 4" x 63 ½".

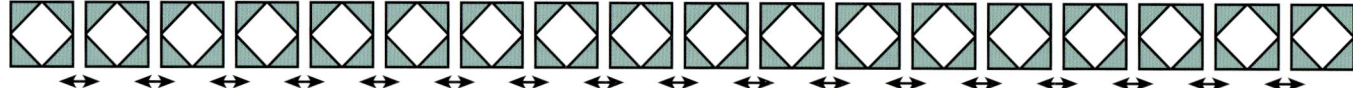

Make two.

Attach side inner borders using the Fabric K1 strips. Attach top and bottom inner borders using the Fabric K2 strips.

Attach Side Middle Borders. Attach Top and Bottom Middle Borders.

Attach side outer borders using the Fabric M1 strips. Attach top and bottom outer borders using the Fabric M2 strips.

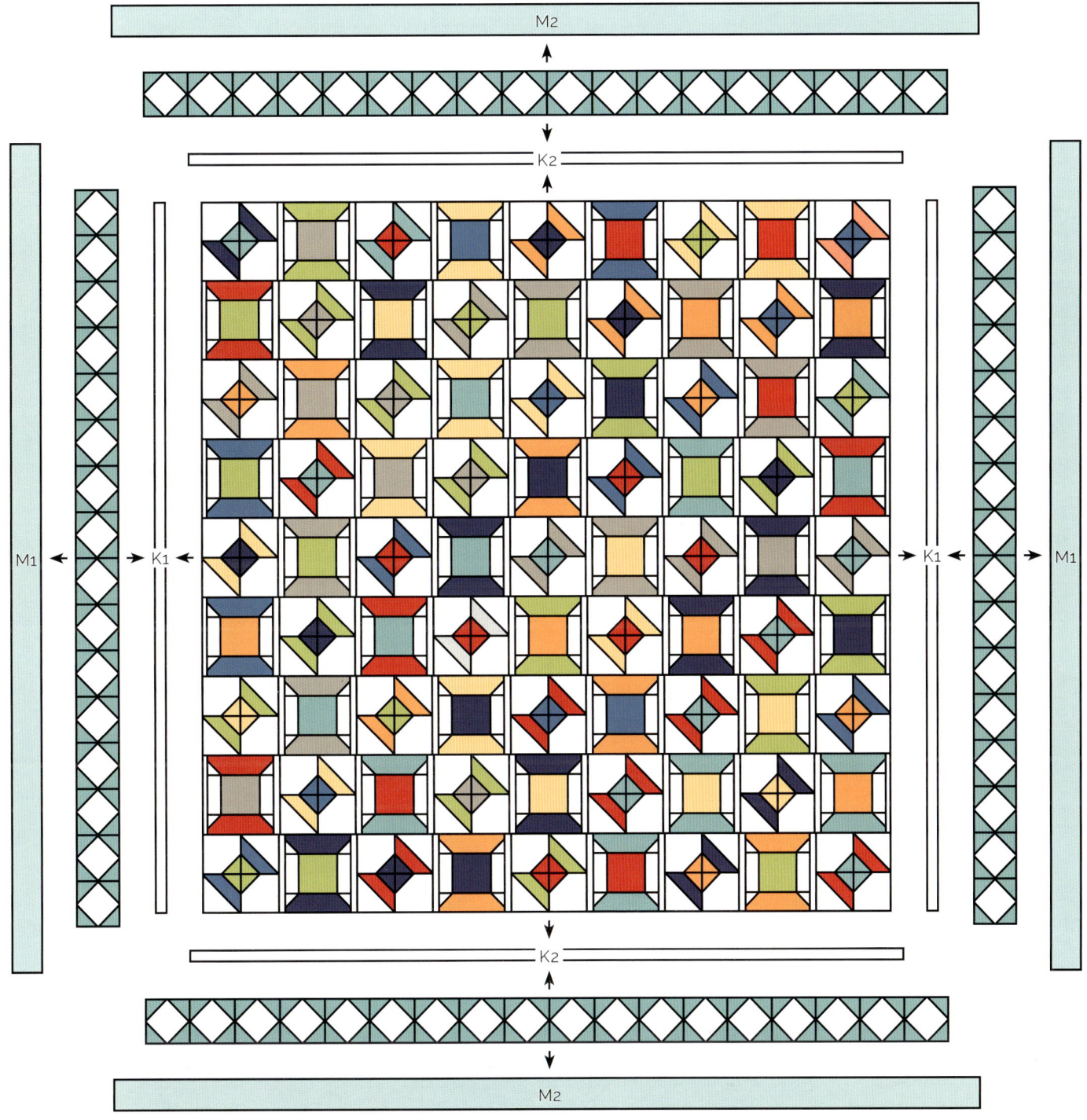

Finishing:

Piece the Fabric N strips end to end for binding.

Quilt and bind as desired.

Carrie's Vintage Spools Quilt

65 ½" x 71 ½"

Designed and Sewn by: Carrie Nelson / Quilted by: Maggi Honeyman (Instagram: @sewmaggi)

Fabric Requirements:

4 yards - Background and Border	
3 - 4" x WOF strips, subcut into: 24 - 4" squares	A
5 - 3 ½" x WOF strips, subcut into: 48 - 3 ½" squares	B
33 - 1 ⅝" x WOF strips, subcut into: 172 - 1 ⅝" x 3 ½" rectangles 344 - 1 ⅝" squares	C D
29 - 1" x WOF strips, subcut into: 172 - 1" x 6 ½" rectangles	E
8 - 3" x WOF strips, sew end to end and subcut into: 2 - 3" x 66 ½" strips 2 - 3" x 65 ½" strips	F1 F2

86 Layer Cake squares - Blocks	
From each 10" square cut: 2 - 2" x 5 ¾" rectangles (172 total)	G

171 Charm Pack squares - Blocks	
From twenty-four 5" squares cut: 1 - 4" square (24 total)	H
From twenty-four 5" squares cut: 2 - 2" squares (48 total) 2 - 2" squares (48 total)	I1 I2
From fifty-seven 5" squares cut: 1 - 3 ½" square (57 total)	J
From twenty-one 5" squares cut: 5 - 1 ½" squares (105 total)	K
From twenty-one 5" squares cut: 4 - 1 ½" squares (84 total)	L
From twenty-four 5" squares cut: 1 - 1 ½" x 3 ½" rectangle (24 total)	M

8 - ⅛ yards - Binding	
From each ⅛ yard cut: 1 - 2 ¼" x WOF strip (8 total)	N

4 ⅝ yards - Backing

Refer to page 18 for Side Vintage Spools Block instructions.

Side Vintage Spools Blocks:

Each Side Vintage Spools Block uses three coordinating prints.

Assemble Block using coordinating fabric. Side Vintage Spools Block should measure 6 ½" x 6 ½".

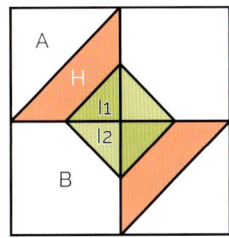

Make twenty-four total.

Refer to page 19 for Straight Vintage Spools Block instructions.

Straight Vintage Spools Blocks:

Each Straight Vintage Spools Block uses two coordinating prints.

Assemble Block using coordinating fabric. Straight Vintage Spools Block should measure 6 ½" x 6 ½".

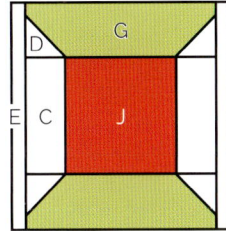

Make fifty-seven total.

Carrie's Vintage Spools Quilt

Three Patch Straight Vintage Spools Blocks:

Each Three Patch Straight Vintage Spools Block uses four coordinating prints.

Draw a diagonal line on the wrong side of the Fabric D squares.

With right sides facing, layer a Fabric D square on the bottom left corner of a Fabric G rectangle.

Stitch on the drawn line and trim ¼" away from the seam.

Repeat on the bottom right corner.

Outer Spool Unit should measure 2" x 5 ¾".

Make fifty-eight.

Assemble Unit using three different Fabric M rectangles.

Three Patch Inner Spool Unit should measure 3 ½" x 5 ¾".

Make eight.

Assemble Unit using coordinating fabric.

Three Patch Straight Vintage Spools Unit should measure 5 ¾" x 6 ½".

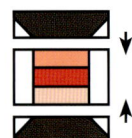 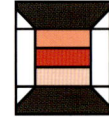

Make eight.

Assemble Block.

TRIM Three Patch Straight Vintage Spools Block to measure 6 ½" x 6 ½".

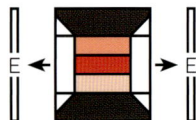 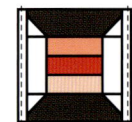 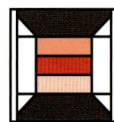

Make eight.

Nine Patch Straight Vintage Spools Blocks:

Each Nine Patch Straight Vintage Spools Block uses three coordinating prints.

Assemble Unit using coordinating fabric. Press open.

Partial Nine Patch Inner Spool Unit should measure 3 ½" x 3 ½".

Make twenty-one.

Assemble Unit.

Nine Patch Inner Spool Unit should measure 3 ½" x 5 ¾".

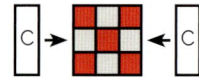 

Make twenty-one.

Assemble Unit using coordinating fabric.

Nine Patch Straight Vintage Spools Unit should measure 5 ¾" x 6 ½".

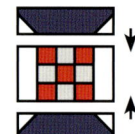 

Make twenty-one.

Assemble Block.

TRIM Nine Patch Straight Vintage Spools Block to measure 6 ½" x 6 ½".

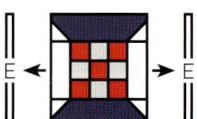  

Make twenty-one.

Quilt Center:

Assemble Quilt Center. Press open.

Quilt Center should measure 60 ½" x 66 ½".

Carrie's Vintage Spools Quilt

Border:

Attach side borders using the Fabric F1 strips.

Attach top and bottom borders using the Fabric F2 strips.

Finishing:

Piece the Fabric N strips end to end to make the scrappy binding. Press open for less bulk.

You will need approximately 304 inches for binding.

Quilt as desired.

Vintage Spools Sewing Machine Cover

27 ½" x 33 ½"

Designed by: Joanna Figueroa / Sewn and Quilted by: Anna Dineen (Instagram: @mywanderingpath)

Fabric Requirements:

20 Low Volume Layer Cake squares - Blocks	
From ten 10" squares cut:	
1 - 4" square (10 total)	A
2 - 3 ½" squares (20 total)	B
From ten 10" squares cut:	
2 - 1 ⅝" x 3 ½" rectangles (20 total)	C
4 - 1 ⅝" squares (40 total)	D
2 - 1" x 6 ½" rectangles (20 total)	E

30 Print Charm Pack squares - Blocks	
From ten 5" squares cut:	
1 - 4" square (10 total)	F
From ten 5" squares cut:	
4 - 2" squares (40 total)	G
From ten 5" squares cut:	
1 - 3 ½" square (10 total)	H

10 Print Layer Cake squares - Blocks	
From each 10" squares cut:	
2 - 2" x 5 ¾" rectangles (20 total)	I

⅜ yard - Border	
4 - 2" x WOF strips, subcut into:	
2 - 2" x 30 ½" strips	J
2 - 2" x 27 ½" strips	K

½ yard - Sewing Machine Cover Ties and Binding	
1 - 2" x WOF strip, subcut into:	
4 - 2" x 10 ½" rectangles	L
4 - 2 ¼" x WOF strips	M

Craft Size - Batting
1 - 31 ½" x 37 ½" rectangle

⅞ yard - Backing
1 - 31 ½" x 37 ½" rectangle

Refer to page 18 for Side Vintage Spools Block instructions.

Side Vintage Spools Blocks:

Assemble Block using coordinating fabric.
Side Vintage Spools Block should measure 6 ½" x 6 ½".

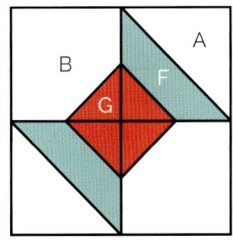

Make ten total.

Refer to page 19 for Straight Vintage Spools Block instructions.

Straight Vintage Spools Blocks:

Assemble Block using coordinating fabric.
Straight Vintage Spools Block should measure 6 ½" x 6 ½".

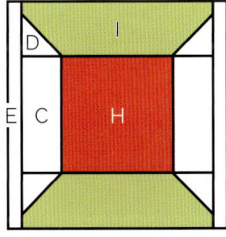

Make ten total.

Meet Anna Dineen

Meeting Anna was simply meant to be. Carrie stumbled upon her Instagram before meeting her in person, and Joanna discovered her shortly after that through her blog, www.mywanderingpath.com. They both connected with Anna for the same reasons - a love of quilting and making, and shared ideas about life perspectives. Plus, how can you not love someone who describes themselves as a "Southern girl in exile in Texas"?

Vintage Spools Sewing Machine Cover

Sewing Machine Cover Center:

Assemble Sewing Machine Cover Center. Press toward Straight Vintage Spools Blocks.

Sewing Machine Cover Center should measure 24 ½" x 30 ½".

Border:

Attach side borders using the Fabric J strips.

Attach top and bottom borders using the Fabric K strips.

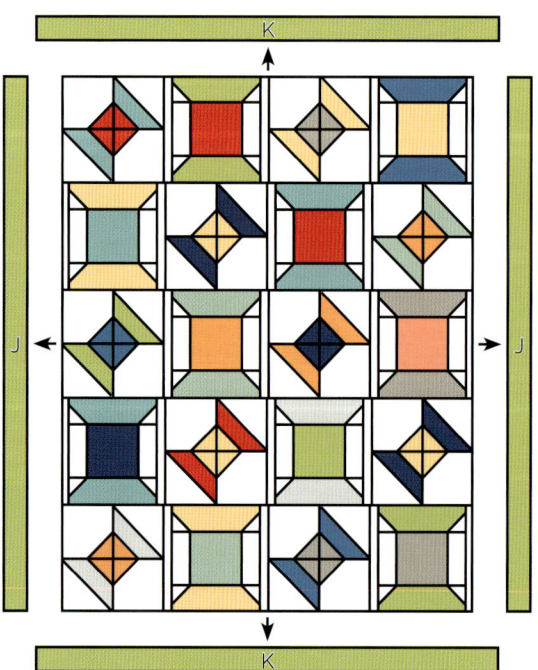

Quilted Sewing Machine Cover Top:

Layer the Sewing Machine Cover Top, the Batting and the Backing.

Quilt as desired. Trim excess Batting and Backing.

Baste ⅛" around the inside of the Quilted Sewing Machine Cover Top.

Quilted Sewing Machine Cover Top will shrink after quilting.

Sewing Machine Cover Ties:

With the right side facing down, fold one short side of a Fabric L strip ¼" in from the edge. Press.

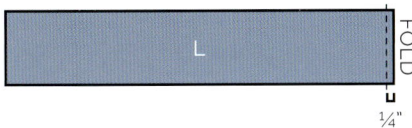

Make four.

Fold a Fabric L strip in half, lengthwise. Press.

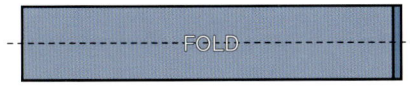

Make four.

Open and fold each edge in to meet the fold mark in the middle. Press.

Fold in half again. Press.

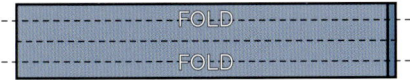

Make four.

Topstitch ⅛" away from the open edge to create a Sewing Machine Cover Tie.

Make four.

Finishing:

We recommend using your sewing machine as a placement guide.

In our sample we placed the ties 10 ½" from the edge.

Matching raw edges, place the Sewing Machine Cover Ties on the back of the Quilted Sewing Machine Cover Top. Pin in place.

Baste ⅛" away from the edges to secure the Sewing Machine Cover Ties in place.

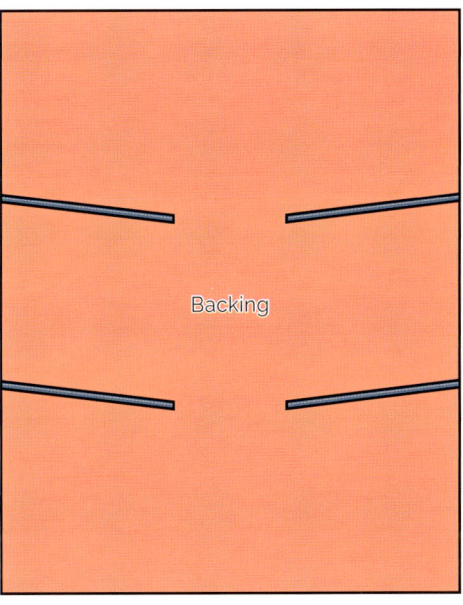

Piece the Fabric M strips end to end for binding. Bind as desired.

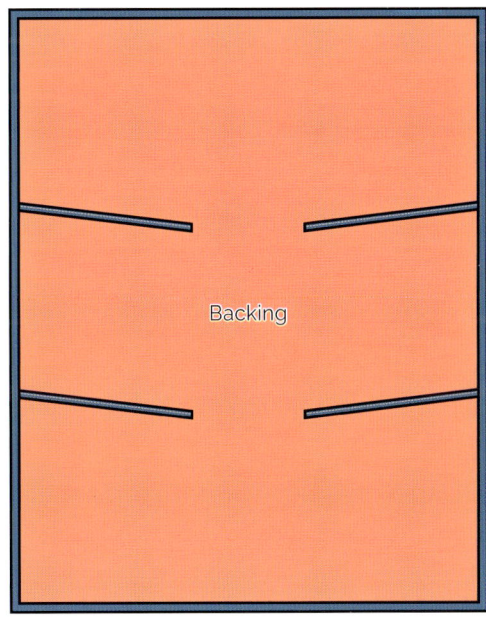

Vintage Spools Pillow

14" x 26"

Designed, Sewn and Quilted by: Joanna Figueroa

We have pillow finishing instructions and tips on page 14!

Fabric Requirements:

½ yard - Background	
1 - 4" x WOF strip, subcut into: 8 - 4" squares	A
2 - 3 ½" x WOF strips, subcut into: 16 - 3 ½" squares	B

35 Charm Pack squares - Blocks and Border	
From eight 5" squares cut: 1 - 4" square (8 total)	C
From eight 5" squares cut: 4 - 2" squares (32 total)	D
From one 5" square cut: 4 - 1 ½" squares (4 total)	E
From eighteen 5" squares cut: 4 - 1 ½" squares (72 total)	F

1 Layer Cake square - Blocks	
From the 10" square cut: 12 - 2" squares	G

Refer to page 18 for Side Vintage Spools Block instructions.

Side Vintage Spools Blocks:

Assemble Block using coordinating fabric.

Side Vintage Spools Block should measure 6 ½" x 6 ½".

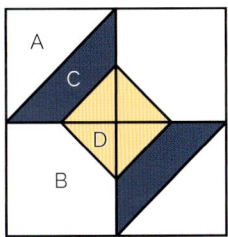

Make eight total.

Draw a line on the wrong side of the Fabric G squares.

With right sides facing, layer a Fabric G square on the bottom right corner of a Side Vintage Spools Block.

Stitch on the drawn line and trim ¼" away from the seam.

Side Vintage Spools Block One should measure 6 ½" x 6 ½".

Make two total.

With right sides facing, layer a Fabric G square on the bottom left corner of a Side Vintage Spools Block.

Stitch on the drawn line and trim ¼" away from the seam.

Side Vintage Spools Block Two should measure 6 ½" x 6 ½".

Make two total.

With right sides facing, layer Fabric G squares on the bottom left and right corners of a Side Vintage Spools Block.

Stitch on the drawn lines and trim ¼" away from the seam.

Side Vintage Spools Block Three should measure 6 ½" x 6 ½".

Make four total.

Pillow Center:

Assemble Pillow Center. Press open.

Pillow Center should measure 12 ½" x 24 ½".

Border:

Assemble Border using twelve Fabric F squares. Press open.

Side Border should measure 1 ½" x 12 ½".

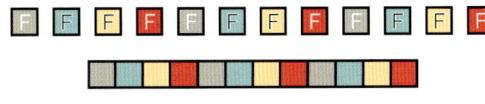

Make two.

Vintage Spools Pillow

Assemble Border using two Fabric E squares and twenty-four Fabric F squares. Press open.
Top and Bottom Border should measure 1 ½" x 26 ½".

Make two.

Attach Side Borders.
Attach Top and Bottom Borders.

Vintage Spools Pincushion

4" × 4"

Designed by: Joanna Figueroa
Sewn and Quilted by: Cynthia Bird
(Instagram: @cynthia.bird)

We have pincushion finishing instructions and tips on page 12!

Fabric Requirements:

1 Layer Cake square - Background	
From the 10" square cut:	
1 - 2 ¼" square	A
2 - 1 ¾" squares	B
12 - 1" squares	C
3 Charm Pack squares - Block and Border	
From one 5" square cut:	
1 - 2 ¼" square	D
From one 5" square cut:	
4 - 1" squares	E
From one 5" square cut:	
12 - 1" squares	F
4 Charm Pack squares - Pieced Backing	
From each 5" square cut:	
2 - 1" x 4 ½" rectangles (8 total)	G
Scraps - Batting	
2 - 4 ½" squares	

Small Vintage Spools Block:

Draw a diagonal line on the wrong side of the Fabric D square.

With right sides facing, layer the Fabric D square with the Fabric A square.

Stitch ¼" from each side of the drawn line.

Cut apart on the marked line.

TRIM Half Square Triangle Unit to measure 1 ¾" x 1 ¾".

Make two.

Draw a diagonal line on the wrong side of the Fabric E squares.

With right sides facing, layer a Fabric E square on the bottom right corner of a Half Square Triangle Unit.

Stitch on the drawn line and trim ¼" away from the seam.

Outer Spool Unit should measure 1 ¾" x 1 ¾".

Make two.

With right sides facing, layer a Fabric E square on the bottom left corner of a Fabric B square.

Stitch on the drawn line and trim ¼" away from the seam.

Inner Spool Unit should measure 1 ¾" x 1 ¾.

Make two.

Assemble Block. Press open.

Small Vintage Spools Block should measure 3" x 3".

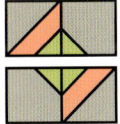 

Make one.

Border:

Assemble Border. Press open.

Side Border should measure 1" x 3".

Make two.

Assemble Border. Press open.

Top and Bottom Border should measure 1" x 4".

Make two.

Attach Side Borders. Attach Top and Bottom Borders. Press open.

Vintage Spools Pincushion Top should measure 4" x 4".

   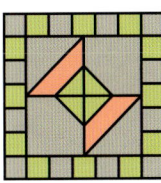

Pieced Backing:

Assemble Pieced Backing. Press open.

Pieced Backing should measure 4 ½" x 4 ½".

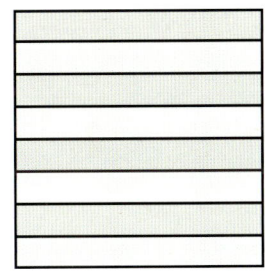

Chapter 2:
Nine Across

by Carrie Nelson

"Like red lipstick, a little black dress and pearl earrings, you can't go wrong with a nine patch quilt. The beauty is in the simplicity.

Nine Across started with the nine patch blocks (scrappy, of course) and a diagonal setting. To mix it up a bit, a second block was added – a Greek Cross that looked like a button in this setting. The Minick & Simpson fabrics were a perfect fit, though I am already thinking of additional fabric options."

Carrie

"Mixing solids and lots and lots of low volume cream prints is one of my favorite things to do when I don't have a pattern deadline. Seriously! So it was kind of a no-brainer when Carrie proposed this design as one of her choices. Nine patches, solids and creamy low volumes ... oh my ... it was a match made in heaven, if you ask me."

Joanna

Nine Across Block

Small - 5" x 5" unfinished
Large - 6 ½" x 6 ½" unfinished

Small Block Cutting Instructions:

Description		Cutting
Background	A	4 - 2" squares
Print	B	5 - 2" squares

Large Block Cutting Instructions:

Description		Cutting
Background	A	4 - 2 ½" squares
Print	B	5 - 2 ½" squares

Piecing Instructions:

Assemble Unit.

Outer Nine Across Unit should measure:

      Small - 2" x 5"
      Large - 2 ½" x 6 ½"

Make two.

- -

Assemble Unit.

Inner Nine Across Unit should measure:

      Small - 2" x 5"
      Large - 2 ½" x 6 ½"

Make one.

- -

Assemble Block. Press open.

Nine Across Block should measure:

      Small - 5" x 5"
      Large - 6 ½" x 6 ½"

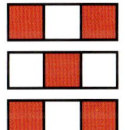 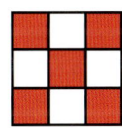

Make one.

Off the Cuff ...
CLIPPING SEAMS

« Carrie »

I used to think this was nuts, it went against all of the "quilting rules". Then someone compared it to clipping seams on collars and sleeves when making garments. That was a light bulb moment ... duh. There are times when two seams will be pressed in the same direction, or parts of the same seam are best pressed in opposite directions. Clipping into the seam to flip it in the other direction, or to open it up, has the best results. (I do this for sawtooth star blocks.)

« Joanna »

Somehow I have always been a bit scared to try this method, but I see all of my sewing ladies doing it all around me. My favorite one to see is the little center clipped "pinwheel" in the middle of a star block. Moment of truth? I only clip seams when I mess up and realize after pressing that half the seam is going one way and half is going the other way. (Can't believe I'm admitting to this out loud in print!) It is only then that I will clip a seam, mostly to save myself the embarrassment of what the quilter will see when she receives my quilt!

Button Block

A
E
C
B
D

Small - 5" x 5" unfinished
Large - 6 ½" x 6 ½" unfinished

Small Block Cutting Instructions:

Description		Cutting
Background	A	2 - 2 ⅜" squares
	B	1 - 1 ¼" x 10" rectangle
Print	C	2 - 2 ⅜" squares
	D	1 - 2" square
	E	1 - 1 ¼" x 10" rectangle

Large Block Cutting Instructions:

Description		Cutting
Background	A	2 - 2 ⅞" squares
	B	1 - 1 ½" x 11" rectangle
Print	C	2 - 2 ⅞" squares
	D	1 - 2 ½" square
	E	1 - 1 ½" x 11" rectangle

Piecing Instructions:

Draw a diagonal line on the wrong side of the Fabric A squares.

With right sides facing, layer a Fabric A square with a Fabric C square.

Stitch ¼" from each side of the drawn line.

Cut apart on the marked line.

Half Square Triangle Unit should measure:

Small - 2" x 2"
Large - 2 ½" x 2 ½"

 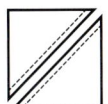

Make four.

Assemble the Fabric E rectangle and the Fabric B rectangle.

Button Strip Set should measure:

Small - 2" x 10"
Large - 2 ½" x 11"

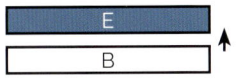 

Make one.

Subcut the Button Strip Set into four squares.

Button Unit should measure:

Small - 2" x 2"
Large - 2 ½" x 2 ½"

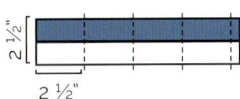

Make four.

Assemble Block. Press open.

Button Block should measure:

Small - 5" x 5"
Large - 6 ½" x 6 ½"

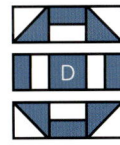 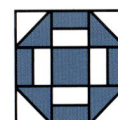

Make one.

Off the Cuff ...
PRESSING

« Joanna »

Pressing directions are one of those things I know people feel very strongly about and something I have completely changed my mind on over the years! I started off as a diligent "press to the dark" or "press to the side with fewer seams" kind of girl, and sometimes I still go there if the fabric really wants to do that. But in general, I have completely switched over to the "pressing seams open" camp. I find that my blocks are more accurate and lie flatter. I struggle with those smaller sections less and in general, I like the outcome more!

« Carrie »

Pressing to one side was how we were taught, and I followed that for many years. I know there were good reasons why we pressed seams to one side, but with better fabric, batting, thread and sewing machines, now we can do what works best. There are seams I press to one side and seams I press open.

Pinning is a must when seams are pressed open. And remember, pressing open can make a block a little bit bigger.

Carrie's Nine Across Quilt

81" x 81"

Designed by: Carrie Nelson / Sewn by: Anna Dineen (Instagram: @mywanderingpath)
Quilted by: Carrie Straka (Instagram: @redvelvet_quilts)

Fabric Requirements:

3 ½ yards - Background and Border	
2 - 10" x WOF strips, subcut into:	
8 - 10" squares	A
7 - 6 ½" x WOF strips, subcut into:	
37 - 6 ½" squares	B
from the remainder of strip cut:	
2 - 5 ¼" squares	C
6 - 2 ⅞" x WOF strips, subcut into:	
72 - 2 ⅞" squares	D
9 - 1 ½" x WOF strips, subcut into:	
36 - 1 ½" x 10 ½" rectangles	E
9 - 2 ½" x WOF strips, sew end to end and subcut into:	
2 - 2 ½" x 77" strips	F1
2 - 2 ½" x 81" strips	F2
18 Low Volume Fat Eighths - Nine Across Blocks	
From each 9" x 21" rectangle cut:	
1 - 2 ½" x 21" strip (18 total)	G
2 - 2 ½" x 10 ½" rectangles (36 total)	H
18 Red Fat Eighths - Nine Across Blocks	
From each 9" x 21" rectangle cut:	
2 - 2 ½" x 21" strips (36 total)	I
1 - 2 ½" x 10 ½" rectangle (18 total)	J
12 Blue Fat Quarters - Button Blocks	
From each 18" x 21" rectangle cut:	
6 - 2 ⅞" squares (72 total)	K
3 - 2 ½" squares (36 total)	L
3 - 1 ½" x 10 ½" rectangles (36 total)	M
1 yard - Binding	
354" of 2 ¼" bias binding strips	N
7 ⅝ yards - Backing	

Nine Across Blocks:

Each Nine Across Block uses two fat eighths (set).

Assemble two matching Fabric I strips and one coordinating Fabric G strip.

Long Strip Set should measure 6 ½" x 21".

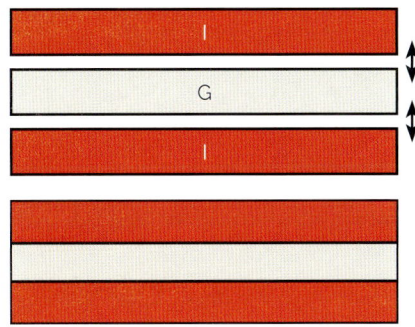

Make one from each set.
Make eighteen total.

Subcut each Long Strip Set into eight 2 ½" x 6 ½" rectangles.

Outer Nine Across Unit should measure 2 ½" x 6 ½".

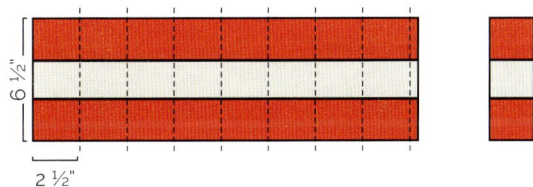

Make eight from each set.
Make one hundred forty-four total.

Assemble two matching Fabric H rectangles and one coordinating Fabric J rectangle.

Short Strip Set should measure 6 ½" x 10 ½".

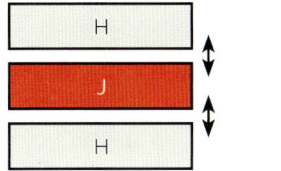

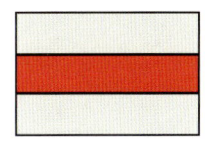

Make one from each set.
Make eighteen total.

Carrie's Nine Across Quilt

Off the Cuff ...
STRIP SETS

« Joanna »

Some things you just have to learn the hard way. When we all started designing quilts with Jelly Rolls, I noticed a lot of variation in my students' work and some wonky piecing in my own too. I quickly realized that sewing several strips together in the same direction would quickly lead to stretched out and less accurately pieced sections. All I needed to do was flip the direction in which I was sewing the strips for a much better outcome. It's one of those million dollar tips that I think makes a huge difference when strip piecing!

« Carrie »

Agreed! This is a game-changing technique. If you're making strip sets for anything, the direction of the stitching needs to be alternated. Figure out a system for joining and marking the starting points and pay attention to it. I would also add that whenever possible, work with strips that are 21" in length instead of the full width of fabric. It makes a difference.

Subcut each Short Strip Set into four 2 ½" x 6 ½" rectangles.

Inner Nine Across Unit should measure 2 ½" x 6 ½".

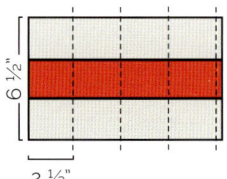 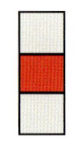

Make four from each set.
Make seventy-two total.

Assemble Block using matching fabric.
Nine Across Block should measure 6 ½" x 6 ½".

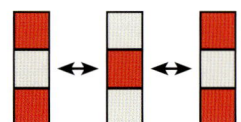 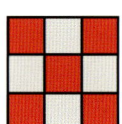

Make four from each set.
Make seventy-two total.

Button Blocks:

Draw a diagonal line on the wrong side of the Fabric D squares.

With right sides facing, layer a Fabric D square with a Fabric K square.

Stitch ¼" from each side of the drawn line.

Cut apart on the marked line.

Half Square Triangle Unit should measure 2 ½" x 2 ½".

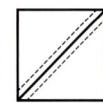 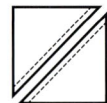

Make twelve from each fat quarter.
Make one hundred forty-four total.

Assemble one Fabric M rectangle and one Fabric E rectangle.

Button Strip Set should measure 2 ½" x 10 ½".

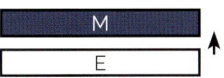 

Make three from each fat quarter.
Make thirty-six total.

Subcut each Button Strip Set into four 2 ½" squares.

Button Unit should measure 2 ½" x 2 ½".

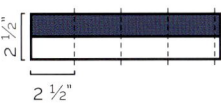

Make twelve from each fat quarter.
Make one hundred forty-four total.

Assemble Block using matching fabric. Press open.

Button Block should measure 6 ½" x 6 ½".

Make three from each fat quarter.
Make thirty-six total.

Setting Triangles:

Cut the Fabric A squares on the diagonal twice.

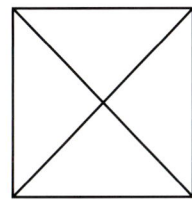 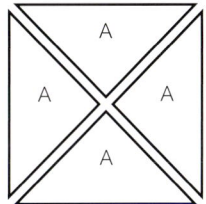

Make thirty-two.

Cut the Fabric C squares on the diagonal once.

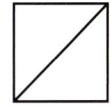 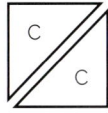

Make four.

Carrie's Nine Across Quilt

Quilt Center:

Assemble Quilt Center. Press rows in opposite directions. Add the Fabric C triangles last.

TRIM Quilt Center to measure 77" x 77".

Border:

Attach side borders using the Fabric F1 strips.

Attach top and bottom borders using the Fabric F2 strips.

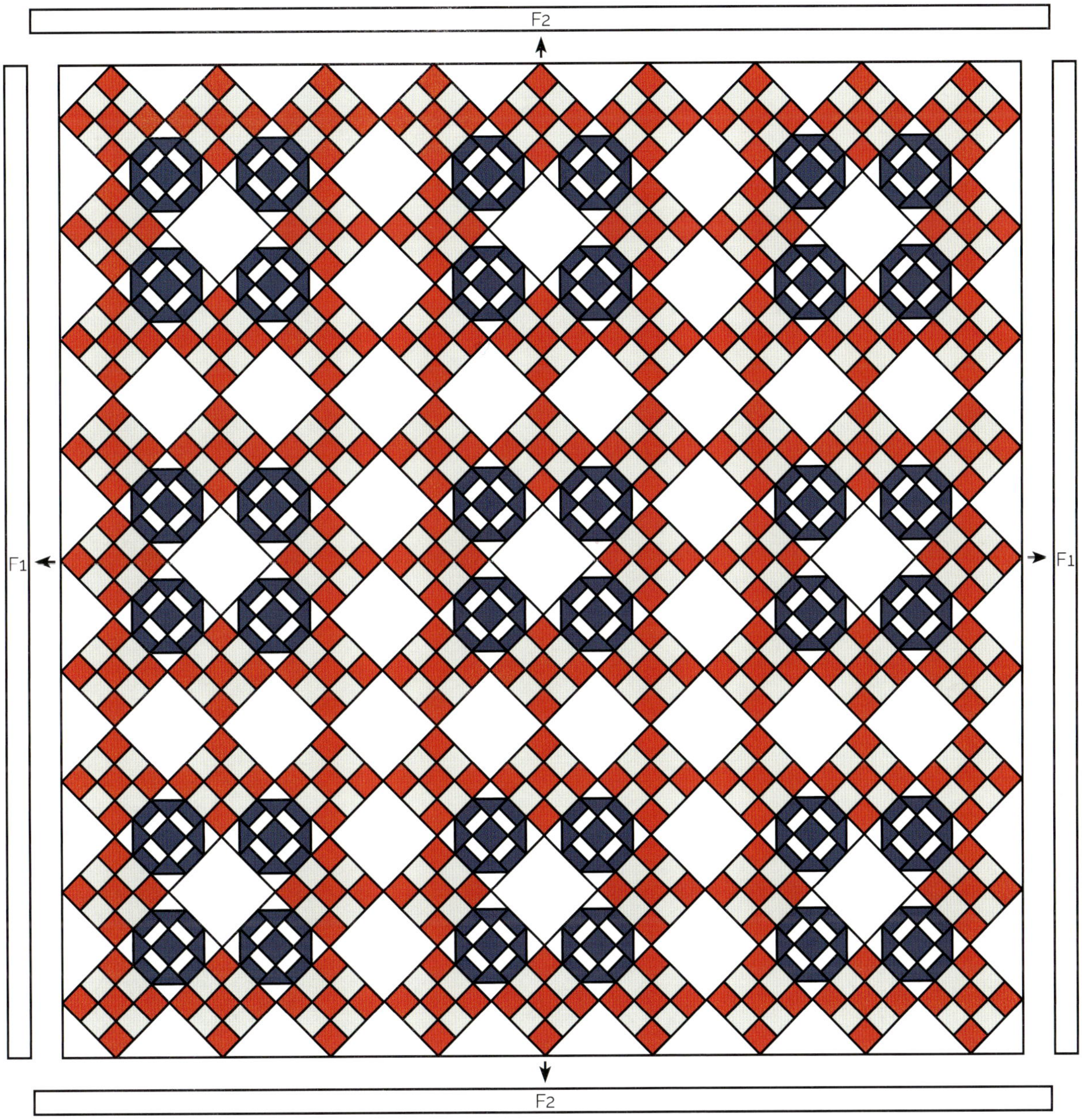

F2

F1

F1

F2

Finishing:

Carrie rounded the corners on her quilt before adding the binding.

Piece the Fabric N strips end to end to make the bias binding. Press open for less bulk.

Quilt as desired.

Joanna's Nine Across Quilt

86" x 86"

Designed by: Joanna Figueroa / Sewn by: Joanna Figueroa and Cheryl Hadley
Quilted by: Marion Bott (Instagram: @bottmarion)

Fabric Requirements:

2 ⅝ yards - Background	
2 - 10" x WOF strips, subcut into: 8 - 10" squares	A

5 - 6 ½" x WOF strips, subcut into:
    28 - 6 ½" squares
    from the remainder of strip cut:
	B

2 - 5 ¼" squares	C
6 - 2 ⅞" x WOF strips, subcut into: 72 - 2 ⅞" squares	D
12 - 1 ½" x WOF strips	E

9 Low Volume Fat Quarters - Nine Across Blocks	
From each 18" x 21" rectangle cut: 8 - 2 ½" x 6" rectangles (72 total)	F
16 - 2 ½" squares (144 total)	G

9 Solid ½ yards - Nine Across Blocks	
From each ½ yard cut 4 - 2 ½" x WOF strips, subcut into:	
16 - 2 ½" x 6" rectangles (144 total)	H
8 - 2 ½" squares (72 total)	I

1 ⅓ yards - Button Blocks	
6 - 2 ⅞" x WOF strips, subcut into: 72 - 2 ⅞" squares	J
3 - 2 ½" x WOF strips, subcut into: 36 - 2 ½" squares	K
12 - 1 ½" x WOF strips	L

9 Low Volume Layer Cake squares - Setting Squares	
From each 10" square cut: 1 - 6 ½" square (9 total)	M

⅔ yard - Inner Border	
9 - 2" x WOF strips, sew end to end and subcut into:	
2 - 2" x 77" strips	N1
2 - 2" x 80" strips	N2

1 ⅛ yards - Outer Border	
10 - 3 ½" x WOF strips, sew end to end and subcut into:	
2 - 3 ½" x 80" strips	O1
2 - 3 ½" x 86" strips	O2

⅞ yard - Binding	
10 - 2 ¼" x WOF strips	P

8 yards - Backing	

Nine Across Blocks:

Each Nine Across Block uses one low volume fabric and one solid fabric (set).

Assemble two matching Fabric H rectangles and one coordinating Fabric F rectangle.

Long Strip Set should measure 6" x 6 ½".

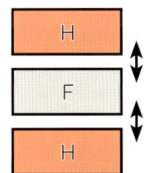 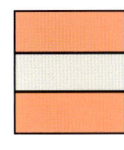

Make eight from each set.
Make seventy-two total.

Subcut each Long Strip Set into two 2 ½" x 6 ½" rectangles.

Outer Nine Across Unit should measure 2 ½" x 6 ½".

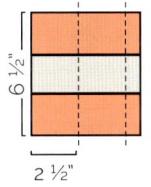 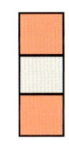

Make sixteen from each set.
Make one hundred forty-four total.

Joanna's Nine Across Quilt

Assemble Unit using coordinating fabric.

Inner Nine Across Unit should measure 2 ½" x 6 ½".

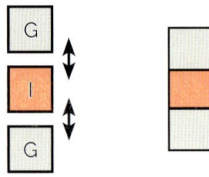

Make eight from each set.
Make seventy-two total.

Assemble Block using matching fabric.

Nine Across Block should measure 6 ½" x 6 ½".

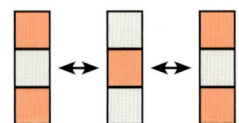 

Make eight from each set.
Make seventy-two total.

Button Blocks:

Draw a diagonal line on the wrong side of the Fabric D squares.

With right sides facing, layer a Fabric D square with a Fabric J square.

Stitch ¼" from each side of the drawn line.

Cut apart on the marked line.

Half Square Triangle Unit should measure 2 ½" x 2 ½".

 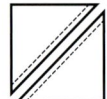 

Make one hundred forty-four.

Assemble one Fabric L strip and one Fabric E strip.

Button Strip Set should measure 2 ½" x WOF.

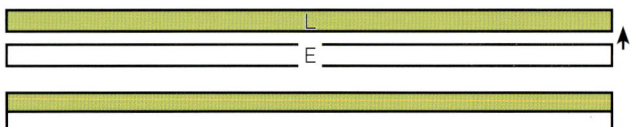

Make twelve.

Subcut each Button Strip Set into twelve 2 ½" squares.

Button Unit should measure 2 ½" x 2 ½".

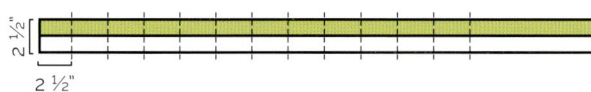

Make one hundred forty-four.

Assemble Block. Press open.

Button Block should measure 6 ½" x 6 ½".

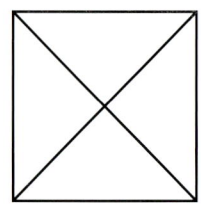 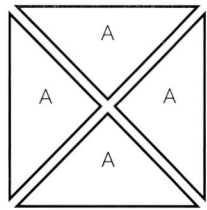

Make thirty-six.

Setting Triangles:

Cut the Fabric A squares on the diagonal twice.

Make thirty-two.

Cut the Fabric C squares on the diagonal once.

Make four.

Quilt Center:

Assemble Quill Center. Press rows in opposite directions. Add the Fabric C triangles last.
TRIM Quilt Center to measure 77" x 77".

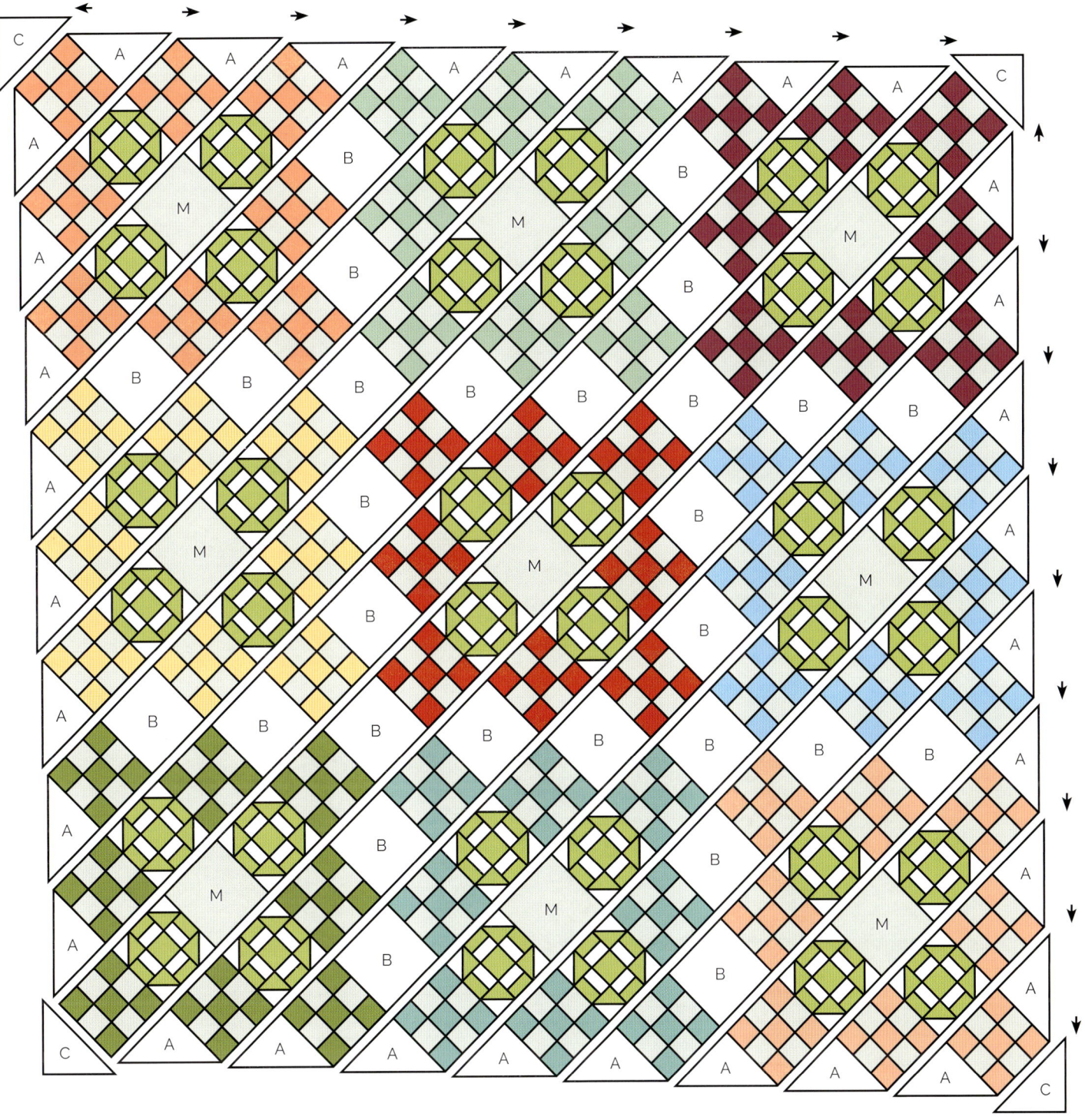

Joanna's Nine Across Quilt

Border:

Attach side inner borders using the Fabric N1 strips. Attach top and bottom inner borders using the Fabric N2 strips.

Attach side outer borders using the Fabric O1 strips. Attach top and bottom outer borders using the Fabric O2 strips.

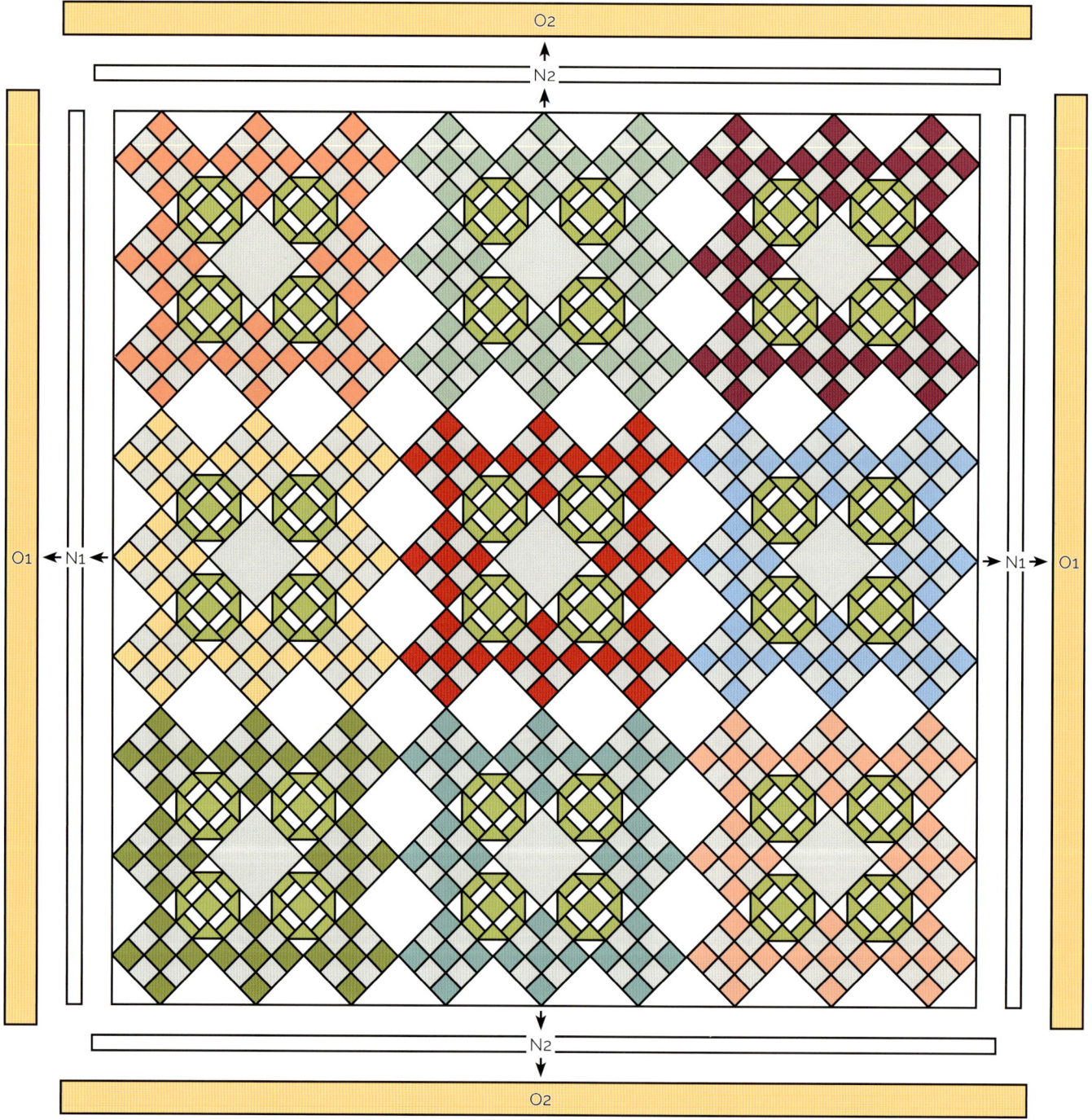

Finishing:

Piece the Fabric P strips end to end for binding.

Quilt and bind as desired.

Nine Across Throw

54 ½" x 69 ½"

Designed by: Joanna Figueroa / Sewn by: Chelsi Stratton (Instagram: @chelsistratton)
Quilted by: Brooke Becker of LadyBelle Fabric (Instagram: @ladybellefabric)

Fabric Requirements:

2 ½ yards - Background and Sashing

3 - 6 ½" x WOF strips, subcut into: 3 - 6 ½" x 33" strips	A
8 - 6 ½" x WOF strips, subcut into: 142 - 2" x 6 ½" rectangles	B
8 - 1 ½" x WOF strips, subcut into: 16 - 1 ½" x 21" strips	C

10 Low Volume Fat Eighths - Nine Across Blocks

From each 9" x 21" rectangle cut:
  1 - 2 ½" x 21" strip (10 total)
  2 - 2 ½" x 10 ½" rectangles (20 total)
	D
	E

10 Solid Fat Quarters - Nine Across Blocks and Binding

From each 18" x 21" rectangle cut:
  2 - 2 ½" x 21" strips (20 total)
  1 - 2 ½" x 10 ½" rectangle (10 total)
  4 - 2 ¼" x 9" rectangles (40 total) for binding
	F
	G
	H

1 ⅜ yards - Button Blocks and Cornerstones

3 - 6 ½" x WOF strips, subcut into: 3 - 6 ½" x 33" strips	I
2 - 2 ½" x WOF strips, subcut into: 32 - 2 ½" squares	J
4 - 2" x WOF strips, subcut into: 80 - 2" squares	K
8 - 1 ½" x WOF strips, subcut into: 16 - 1 ½" x 21" strips	L

One roll of 2" Half Square Triangle Paper by Triangles on a Roll (SKU# H200)

3 - two by eleven sections (22 squares each)

3 ⅝ yards - Backing

Nine Across Blocks:

Each Nine Across Block uses one low volume fabric and one solid fabric (set).

....

Assemble two matching Fabric F strips and one coordinating Fabric D strip.

Long Strip Set should measure 6 ½" x 21".

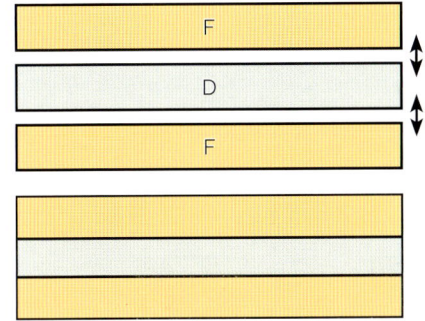

Make one from each set.
Make ten total.

....

Subcut each Long Strip Set into eight 2 ½" x 6 ½" rectangles.

Outer Nine Across Unit should measure
2 ½" x 6 ½".

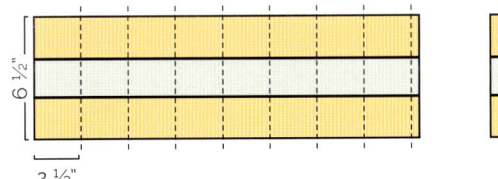

Make eight from each set.
Make eighty total.

....

Assemble two matching Fabric E rectangles and one coordinating Fabric G rectangle.

Short Strip Set should measure 6 ½" x 10 ½".

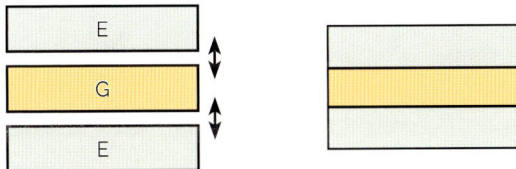

Make one from each set.
Make ten total.

Subcut each Short Strip Set into four 2 ½" x 6 ½" rectangles.

Inner Nine Across Unit should measure 2 ½" x 6 ½".

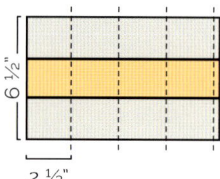 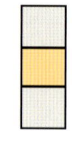

Make four from each set.
Make forty total.

Assemble Block using matching fabric.
Nine Across Block should measure 6 ½" x 6 ½".

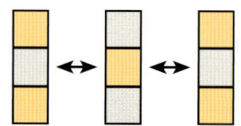 

Make four from each set.
Make forty total.

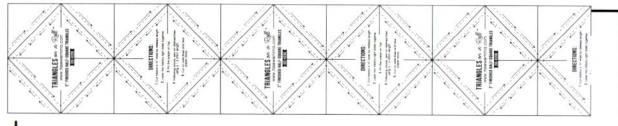

Save your leftover blocks to make a pillow or pincushion!

Button Blocks:

With right sides facing, layer a Fabric A strip with a Fabric I strip.

Place a two by eleven section of 2" Finished Half-Square Triangle Paper on top and pin in place.

Set stitch length to 1.5 and sew on the dotted lines.

Cut apart on the solid lines.

Half Square Triangle Unit should measure 2 ½" x 2 ½".

Make one hundred thirty-two.

Assemble one Fabric L strip and one Fabric C strip.
Button Strip Set should measure 2 ½" x 21".

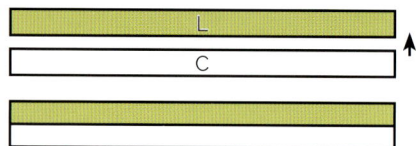

Make sixteen.

Subcut each Button Strip Set into eight 2 ½" squares.
Button Unit should measure 2 ½" x 2 ½".

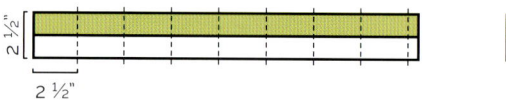

Make one hundred twenty-eight.

Assemble Block. Press open.
Button Block should measure 6 ½" x 6 ½".

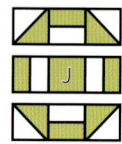 

Make thirty-two.
You will not use all half square triangles.

Quilt Center:

Assemble Quilt Center using Fabric B rectangles for sashing and Fabric K squares for cornerstones. Press toward the sashing.

Quilt Center should measure 54 ½" x 69 ½".

> "Green is the prime color of the world, and that from which its loveliness arises."
>
> *Pedro Calderón de la Barca*

Finishing:

Piece the Fabric H rectangles end to end to make the scrappy binding. Press open for less bulk.
You will need approximately 280 inches for binding.

Quilt as desired.

Nine Across Square Pillow

20" x 20"

Fabric Requirements:

Designed, Sewn and Quilted by: Carrie Nelson

½ yard - Background	
1 - 8 ½" x WOF strip, subcut into:	
2 - 8 ½" squares	A
from the remainder of strip cut:	
2 - 5 ¼" squares	B
1 - 5" square	C
1 - 2 ⅜" x WOF strip, subcut into:	
8 - 2 ⅜" squares	D
1 - 1 ¼" x WOF strip, subcut into:	
4 - 1 ¼" x 10" rectangles	E

8 Blue Layer Cake squares - Blocks	
From each 10" square cut:	
5 - 2" squares (40 total)	F
1 - 2" square (8 total)	G
1 - 1 ¼" x 10" rectangle (8 total)	H

8 Orange Layer Cake squares - Blocks	
From each 10" square cut:	
2 - 2 ⅜" squares (16 total)	I
5 - 2" squares (40 total)	J

We have pillow finishing instructions and tips on page 14!

Refer to page 44 for Small Nine Across Block instructions.

Small Nine Across Blocks:

Each Small Nine Across Block uses two coordinating prints (set).

Assemble Block using coordinating fabric.
Blue Small Nine Across Block should measure 5" x 5".

Make four total.

Assemble Block using coordinating fabric.
Orange Small Nine Across Block should measure 5" x 5".

Make four total.
You will not use all Fabric F and Fabric J squares.

Refer to page 46 for Small Button Block instructions.

Small Button Blocks:

Each Small Button Block uses four blue fabrics and four orange fabrics (set). The remaining fabrics will not be used.

Assemble Block using matching fabric.
Small Button Block should measure 5" x 5".

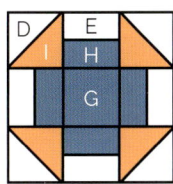

Make one from each set.
Make four total.

Setting Triangles:

Cut the Fabric A squares on the diagonal twice.

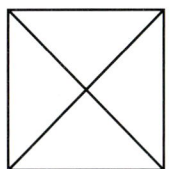 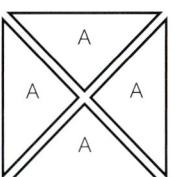

Make eight.

Cut the Fabric B squares on the diagonal once.

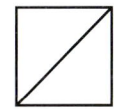 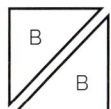

Make four.

Pillow Center:

Assemble Pillow Center. Add the Fabric B triangles last. Press open.
TRIM Pillow Center to measure 20 ½" x 20 ½".

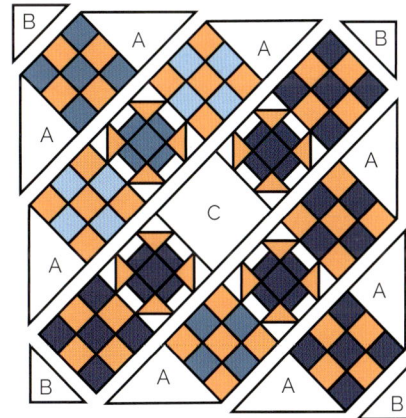

Nine Across Rectangle Pillow

14" x 26"

Designed, Sewn and Quilted by: Carrie Nelson

We have pillow finishing instructions and tips on page 14!

Fabric Requirements:

½ yard - Background

1 - 8 ½" x WOF strip, subcut into:	
2 - 8 ½" squares	A
from the remainder of strip cut:	
2 - 5 ¼" squares	B
1 - 2 ⅜" x WOF strip, subcut into:	
6 - 2 ⅜" squares	C
from the remainder of strip cut:	
3 - 2" squares	D
1 - 1 ¼" x WOF strip, subcut into:	
3 - 1 ¼" x 10" rectangles	E

8 Blue Layer Cake squares - Blocks

From each 10" square cut:	
5 - 2" squares (40 total)	F
1 - 1 ¼" x 10" rectangle (8 total)	G

8 Orange Layer Cake squares - Blocks

From each 10" square cut:	
2 - 2 ⅜" squares (16 total)	H
5 - 2" squares (40 total)	I

Refer to page 44 for Small Nine Across Block instructions.

Small Nine Across Blocks:

Each Small Nine Across Block uses two coordinating prints.

Assemble Block using coordinating fabric.
Blue Small Nine Across Block should measure 5" x 5".

Make six total.

Assemble Block using coordinating fabric.
Orange Small Nine Across Block should measure 5" x 5".

Make two total.
You will not use all Fabric F and Fabric I squares.

Refer to page 46 for Small Button Block instructions.

Small Button Blocks:

Each Small Button Block uses three blue fabrics and three orange fabrics. The remaining fabrics will not be used.

Assemble Block using matching fabric.
Small Button Block should measure 5" x 5".

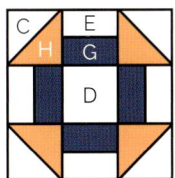

Make three total.

Setting Triangles:

Cut the Fabric A squares on the diagonal twice.

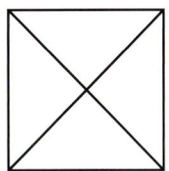 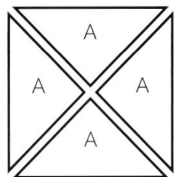

Make eight.

Cut the Fabric B squares on the diagonal once.

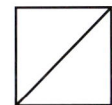 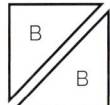

Make four.

Pillow Center:

Assemble Pillow Center. Press open.
TRIM Pillow Center to measure 14 ½" x 26 ½".

Nine Across Pincushion

3" x 3"

Designed, Sewn and Quilted by: Carrie Nelson

Fabric Requirements:

1 Layer Cake square - Background	
From the 10" square cut:	
4 - 1 ½" squares	A
4 - 1" x 1 ½" rectangles	B
Color Coordinating Scraps - Block	
From the scraps cut:	
5 - 1 ½" squares	C
4 - 1" x 1 ½" rectangles	D
Scrap - Backing	
1 - 4" square	
Scraps - Batting	
2 - 4" squares	

We have pincushion finishing instructions and tips on page 12!

"Wooden dough bowls, big glass jars and vintage display boxes – in my home, they're usually filled with pincushions. I happily mix them up by color, fabric style and size ... though one of these days, I hope to have enough to fill a jar with just blue and white pincushions."

Carrie Nelson

Pincushion Center:

Draw a diagonal line on the wrong side of the Fabric A squares.

With right sides facing, layer a Fabric A square with a Fabric C square.

Stitch on the drawn line and trim ¼" away from the seam.

Half Square Triangle Unit should measure 1 ½" x 1 ½".

Make four total.

Assemble Unit.

Two Patch Unit should measure 1 ½" x 1 ½".

Make four total.

....

Assemble Pincushion Center. Press open.

Pincushion Center should measure 3 ½" x 3 ½".

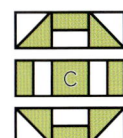 

"I am always drawn to graphic blocks with movement and interesting shapes that can somehow be made in non-traditional ways, like this wagon wheel block. As a designer, it is always a big bonus for me if I can imagine the block done traditionally with a more modern color scheme, and this one definitely fits the bill.

I also love that this block can be made with templates for the traditionalists out there, as well as with a little creative fabric marking for those of us who consider template to be a bad word. I will give you one guess as to which camp I belong? I am so excited to see how Carrie interprets this one with her version!"

Joanna

Chapter 3:
Oregon Trail

by Joanna Figueroa

"With so many quilts dominated by straight lines, any block that has a circular feel to it will always catch my eye. The fact that this could be made with a bit of 'creative fabric marking' made it even more appealing. It was also the perfect block and quilt for a cool bundle Joanna put together last year with blues from Laurie Simpson and Lisa Bongean and Fig Tree oranges.

I wish I had gotten to piece this quilt, because I love how it turned out. It feels traditional and modern at the same time."

Carrie

Oregon Trail Block

10 ½" x 10 ½" unfinished

Cutting Instructions:

Description		Joanna's Stitch & Flip Cutting		Template Cutting
Background	A	4 - 3 ¼" x 4" rectangles	A	4 - Top Outer Corner Units*
	B	4 - 3 ¼" x 4" rectangles	B	4 - Bottom Outer Corner Units*
	C	4 - 2 ½" squares	C	4 - 2 ½" squares
Color #1	D	4 - 4 ½" squares	D	4 - Inner Corner Units*
	E	4 - 2 ½" squares	E	4 - 2 ½" squares
Color #2	F	4 - 2 ½" squares	F	4 - 2 ½" squares
Color #3	G	4 - 2 ½" squares	G	4 - 2 ½" squares
Color #4	H	1 - 2 ½" square	H	1 - 2 ½" square

* Templates are on page 75. Oregon Trail Template Set is available from It's Sew Emma (SKU# ISE-783).

Piecing Instructions:

I originally designed this block using my Stitch & Flip method, but I have also included template instructions if you prefer.

Joanna's Stitch & Flip Method:

On the wrong side of the Fabric A rectangles, mark a dot 2 ⅜" over from the top right corner and another dot 3 ¼" down from the top right corner. Draw a line from dot to dot.

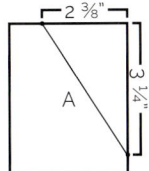

Make four marked Fabric A rectangles.

With right sides facing, layer a Fabric A rectangle on the top right corner of a Fabric D square. Stitch on the drawn line and trim ¼" away from the seam.

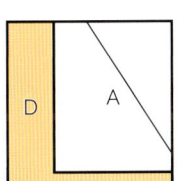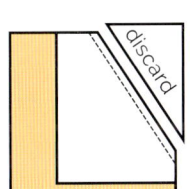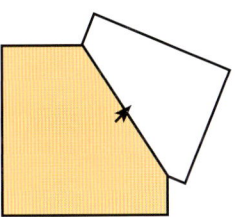

Make four Top Partial Corner Units.

On the wrong side of the Fabric B rectangles, mark a dot 2 ⅜" up from the bottom left corner and another dot 3 ¼" over from the bottom left corner. Draw a line from dot to dot.

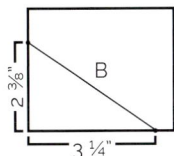

Make four marked Fabric B rectangles.

Oregon Trail Block

With right sides facing, layer a Fabric B rectangle on the bottom left corner of a Top Partial Corner Unit. Stitch on the drawn line and trim ¼" away from the seam.

TRIM Partial Corner Unit to measure 4 ½" x 4 ½".

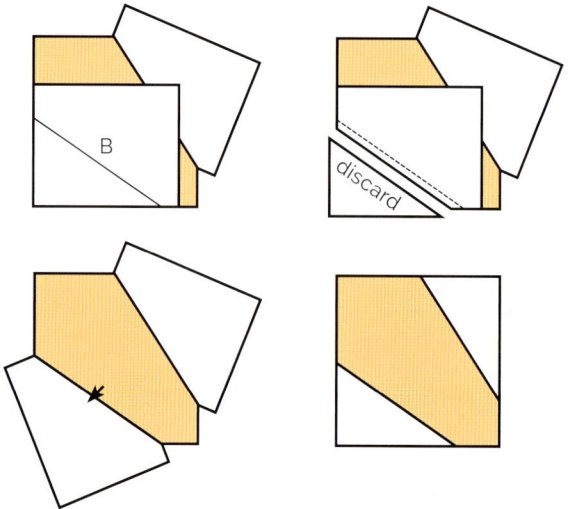

Make four.

Template Method:

With right sides facing, layer a Top Outer Corner Unit with an Inner Corner Unit matching dots. Stitch from dot to dot, using a ¼" seam. Backstitch. Press open.

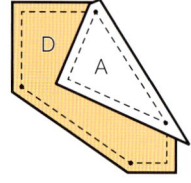 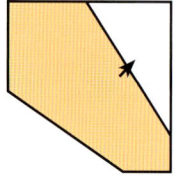

Make four Top Partial Corner Units.

With right sides facing, layer a Bottom Outer Corner Unit with a Top Partial Corner Unit matching dots.

Stitch from dot to dot, using a ¼" seam. Backstitch. Press open.

Partial Corner Unit should measure 4 ½" x 4 ½".

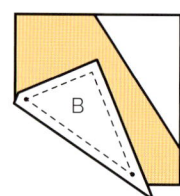 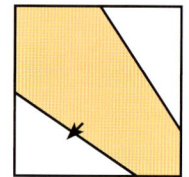

Make four.

Draw a diagonal line on the wrong side of the Fabric C squares and Fabric F squares.

With right sides facing, layer a Fabric C square on the top left corner of a Partial Corner Unit.

Stitch on the drawn line and trim ¼" away from the seam.

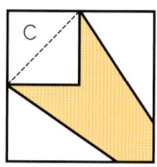 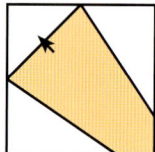

Repeat on the bottom right corner with a Fabric F square.

Corner Unit should measure 4 ½" x 4 ½".

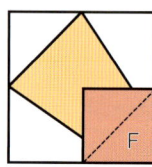 

Make four.

Assemble Unit.

Outer Oregon Trail Unit should measure 4 ½" x 10 ½".

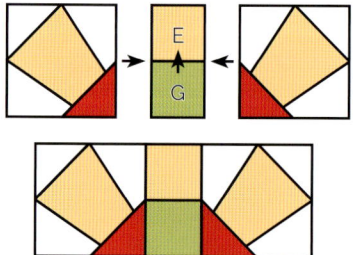

Make two.

Assemble Unit.

Inner Oregon Trail Unit should measure 2 ½" x 10 ½".

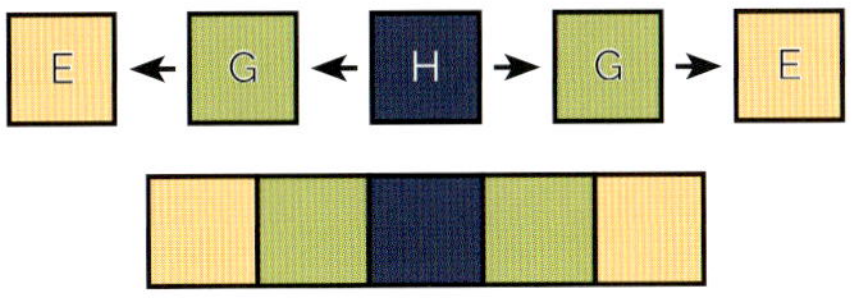
E
G
H
G
E

Make one.

Assemble Block.

Oregon Trail Block should measure 10 ½" x 10 ½".

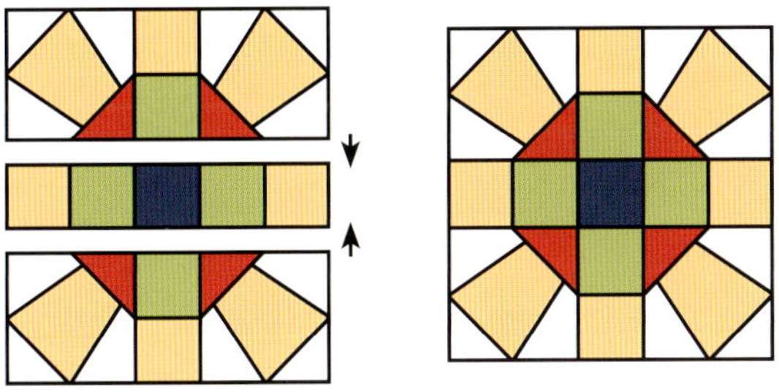

Make one.

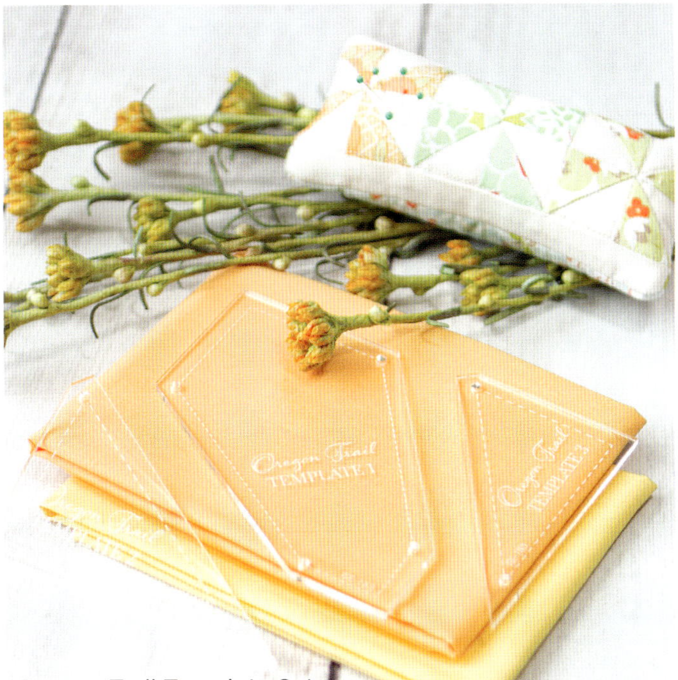
Oregon Trail
TEMPLATE 1
Oregon Trail
TEMPLATE 2

Oregon Trail Template Set
by It's Sew Emma (SKU# ISE-783).

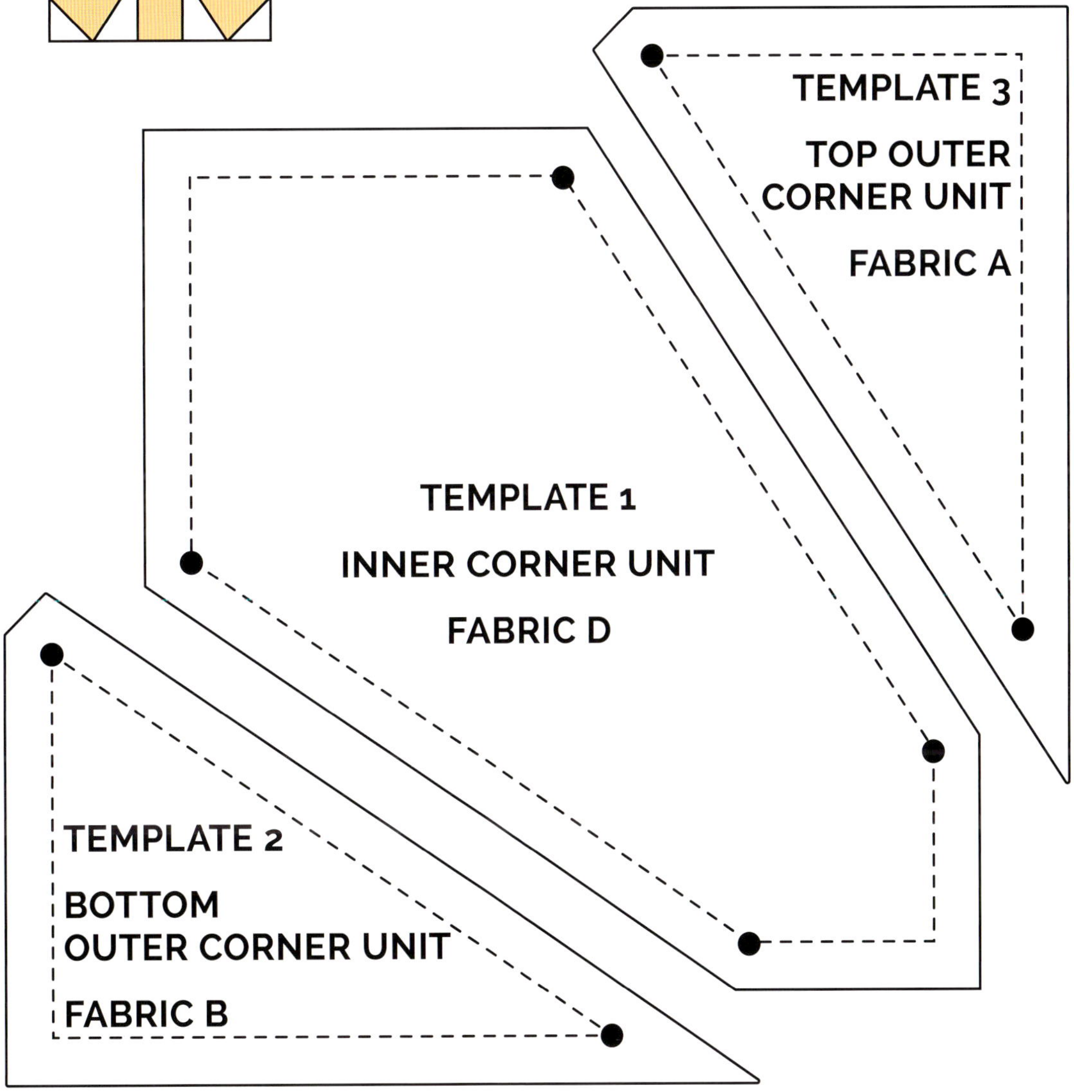
TEMPLATE 3
TOP OUTER CORNER UNIT
FABRIC A
TEMPLATE 1
INNER CORNER UNIT
FABRIC D
TEMPLATE 2
BOTTOM OUTER CORNER UNIT
FABRIC B

Joanna's Oregon Trail Quilt

56 ½" x 68 ½"

Designed by: Joanna Figueroa / Sewn by: Joanna Figueroa and Megan Edgerton
Quilted by: Diana Johnson (Instagram: @quiltedgrammy)

Fabric Requirements:

2 yards - Background	
16 - 3 ¼" x WOF strips, subcut into:	
80 - 3 ¼" x 4" rectangles or Top Outer Corner Units*	A
80 - 3 ¼" x 4" rectangles or Bottom Outer Corner Units*	B
5 - 2 ½" x WOF strips, subcut into:	
80 - 2 ½" squares	C

20 Print Fat Quarters** - Blocks	
From each 18" x 21" rectangle cut:	
4 - 4 ½" squares or Inner Corner Units (80 total)*	D
4 - 2 ½" squares (80 total)	E
4 - 2 ½" squares (80 total)	F
4 - 2 ½" squares (80 total)	G
1 - 2 ½" square (20 total)	H

7 Low Volume Fat Quarters - Sashing	
From each 18" x 21" rectangle cut:	
7 - 2 ½" x 10 ½" rectangles (49 total)	I

1 Fat Quarter - Cornerstones	
From the 18" x 21" rectangle cut:	
30 - 2 ½" squares	J

⅞ yard - Border	
7 - 3 ½" x WOF strips, sew end to end and subcut into:	
2 - 3 ½" x 62 ½" strips	K1
2 - 3 ½" x 56 ½" strips	K2

⅝ yard - Binding	
7 - 2 ¼" x WOF strips	L

3 ¾ yards - Backing	

* Templates are on page 75. Oregon Trail Template Set is available from It's Sew Emma (SKU# ISE-783).

** Print Fat Quarter cutting:

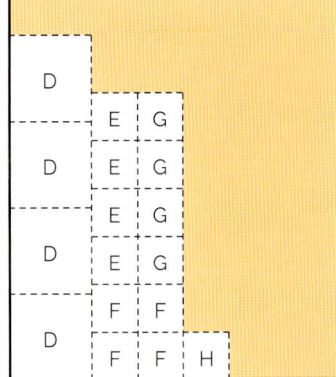

Refer to page 72 for Oregon Trail Block instructions.

Oregon Trail Blocks:

Each Oregon Trail Block uses four coordinating prints.

Assemble Block using coordinating fabric.
Oregon Trail Block should measure 10 ½" x 10 ½".

Make twenty.

Joanna's Oregon Trail Quilt

Quilt Center:

Assemble Quilt Center using Fabric I rectangles for sashing and Fabric J squares for cornerstones. Press toward the sashing.

Quilt Center should measure 50 ½" x 62 ½".

Border:

Attach side borders using the Fabric K1 strips.

Attach top and bottom borders using the Fabric K2 strips.

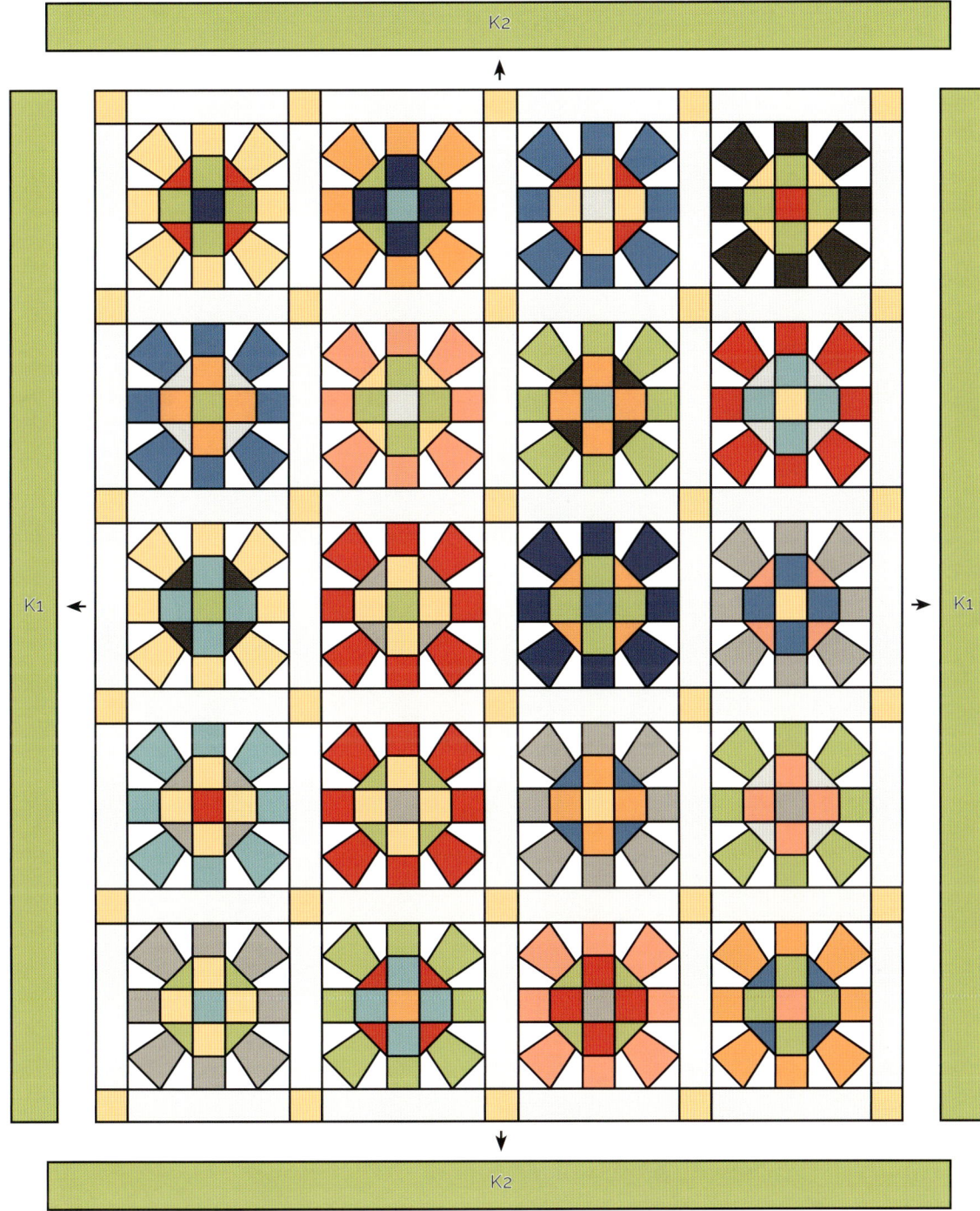

Finishing:

Piece the Fabric L strips end to end for binding.

Quilt and bind as desired.

Carrie's Oregon Trail Quilt

62 ½" x 62 ½"

Designed by: Carrie Nelson / Sewn and Quilted by: Carrie Straka (Instagram: @redvelvet_quilts)

Fabric Requirements:

13 Low Volume Fat Quarters** - Background	
From each 18" x 21" rectangle cut:	
8 - 3 ¼" x 4" rectangles or Top Outer Corner Units* (104 total)	A
8 - 3 ¼" x 4" rectangles or Bottom Outer Corner Units* (104 total)	B
8 - 2 ½" squares (104 total)	C
25 Print Fat Quarters* - Blocks and Cornerstones**	
From each 18" x 21" rectangle cut:	
4 - 4 ½" squares or Inner Corner Units (100 total)*	D
4 - 2 ½" squares (100 total)	E
4 - 2 ½" squares (100 total)	F
4 - 2 ½" squares (100 total)	G
3 - 2 ½" squares (75 total)	H
1 ¼ yards - Sashing	
15 - 2 ½" x WOF strips, subcut into:	
60 - 2 ½" x 10 ½" rectangles	I
⅝ yard - Binding	
7 - 2 ¼" x WOF strips	J
4 ⅛ yards - Backing	

* Templates are on page 75. Oregon Trail Template Set is available from It's Sew Emma (SKU# ISE-783).

Refer to page 72 for Oregon Trail Block instructions.

Oregon Trail Blocks:

Each Oregon Trail Block uses five coordinating prints.

. . . .

Assemble Block using coordinating fabric.
Oregon Trail Block should measure 10 ½" x 10 ½".

Make twenty-five.
You will not use all Fabric A pieces, Fabric B pieces and Fabric C squares.

** Low Volume
Fat Quarter cutting:

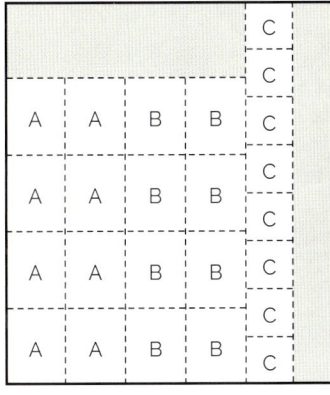

*** Print Fat Quarter cutting:

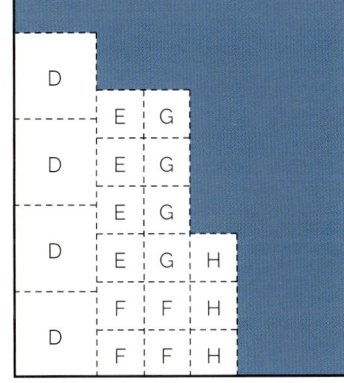

Carrie's Oregon Trail Quilt

Quilt Center:

Assemble Quilt Center using Fabric I rectangles for sashing and Fabric H squares for cornerstones. Press toward the sashing.

Quilt Center should measure 62 ½" x 62 ½".

You will not use all Fabric H squares.

Finishing:

Piece the Fabric J strips end to end for binding.

Quilt and bind as desired.

Oregon Trail Tablerunner

19 ½" x 67 ½"

Designed by: Joanna Figueroa
Sewn by: Susan Ache (Instagram: @yardgrl60) / Quilted by: Susan Rogers (Instagram: @suziquilt)

Fabric Requirements:

⅔ yard - Background

4 - 3 ¼" x WOF strips, subcut into:	
20 - 3 ¼" x 4" rectangles or Top Outer Corner Units*	A
20 - 3 ¼" x 4" rectangles or Bottom Outer Corner Units*	B
2 - 2 ½" x WOF strips, subcut into:	
20 - 2 ½" squares	C

5 Print Fat Eighths** - Blocks

From each 9" x 21" rectangle cut:	
4 - 4 ½" squares or Inner Corner Units (20 total)*	D
4 - 2 ½" squares (20 total)	E

15 Print Scraps - Blocks

From five scraps cut:	
4 - 2 ½" squares (20 total)	F
From five scraps cut:	
4 - 2 ½" squares (20 total)	G
From five scraps cut:	
1 - 2 ½" square (5 total)	H

4 Low Volume Fat Eighths*** - Sashing and Cornerstones

From each 9" x 21" rectangle cut:	
4 - 2 ½" x 10 ½" rectangles (16 total)	I
3 - 2 ½" squares (12 total)	J

⅝ yard - Border

1 - 3" x WOF strip, subcut into:	
2 - 3" x 14 ½" strips	K
4 - 3" x WOF strips, sew end to end and subcut into:	
2 - 3" x 67 ½" strips	L

½ yard - Binding

5 - 2 ¼" x WOF strips	M

2 ¼ yards - Backing

* Templates are on page 75. Oregon Trail Template Set is available from It's Sew Emma (SKU# ISE-783).

** Print Fat Eighth cutting:

*** Low Volume Fat Eighth cutting:

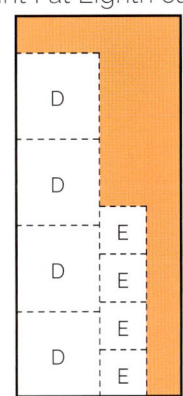

Refer to page 72 for Oregon Trail Block instructions.

Oregon Trail Blocks:

Each Oregon Trail Block uses four coordinating prints.

Assemble Block using coordinating fabric.
Oregon Trail Block should measure 10 ½" x 10 ½".

Make five.

Oregon Trail Tablerunner

Tablerunner Center:

Assemble Tablerunner Center using Fabric I rectangles for sashing and Fabric J squares for cornerstones. Press toward the sashing.

Tablerunner Center should measure 14 ½" x 62 ½".

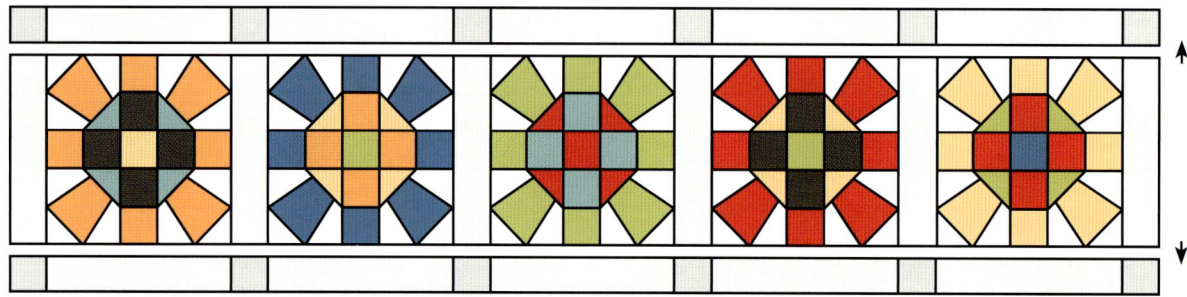

Border:

Attach side borders using the Fabric K strips.

Attach top and bottom borders using the Fabric L strips.

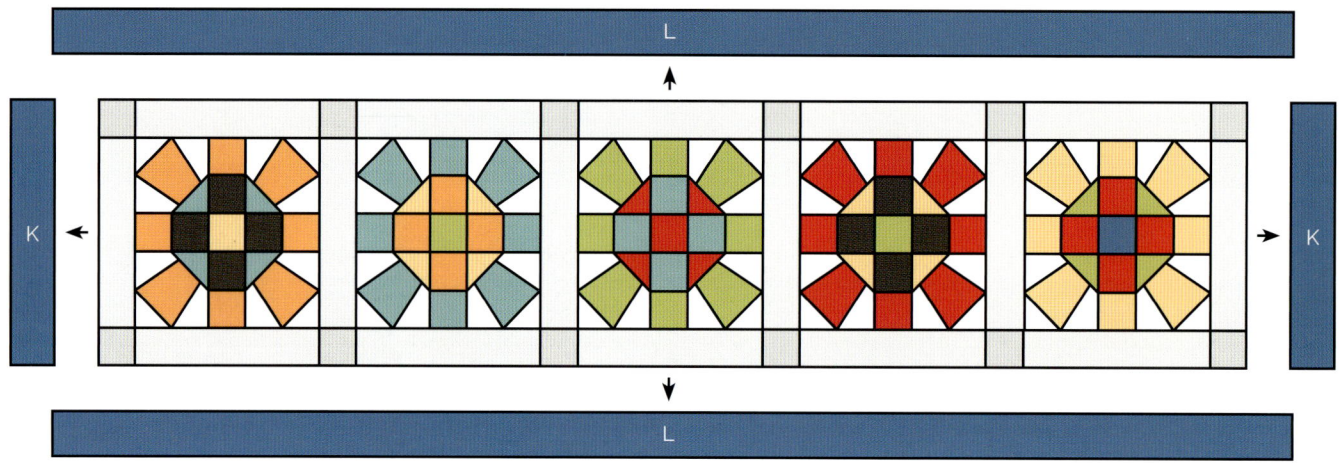

Finishing:

Piece the Fabric M strips end to end for binding.

Quilt and bind as desired.

Meet Susan Ache

While Carrie met Susan at Quilt Market many years ago, both Joanna and Carrie really got to know her as @yardgrl60 on Instagram. Pictures of her stash are legendary, and her home is chock-full of fabulous quilts tucked in every nook and cranny. She contributes to many publications and has several books with Martingale. Joanna and Carrie don't really think she ever sleeps, and wonder how she gets so much quilting done.

Off the Cuff ...
BINDING

« Carrie »

With few exceptions, I cut binding strips at 2" wide. Whether the strips are cut on the bias or straight of grain depends on the fabric. I originally learned that bias binding was the preferred cut for a number of valid reasons. I now use the cut that best suits the fabric being used to get a desired look. Stripes, diagonal plaids and leftover Jelly Roll strips are cut on the straight of grain. Plaids and checks that are woven or printed on the straight of grain are cut on the bias.

« Joanna »

To be honest, I didn't even know there were so many different ways to cut binding and so many different preferences on widths until just recently! I have always cut my binding at 2 ¼" and joined the strips on the diagonal, and seldom cut them on the bias unless, like Carrie, I really wanted it for the design appeal. Since I basically taught myself to quilt from a book, I am not even sure what the "standard" binding size is! I do always use bias binding when I am making scallops or circular binding, but even then I have learned that it doesn't have to be a true 45° bias. Anything near that will be just fine since the fabric will stretch once it's on a significant bias.

Chapter 4:
Pirouette

by Carrie
Nelson

"If I made a list of my favorite 100 quilt blocks, it's a safe bet that 114 of them would have triangles. (Seriously, could you limit yourself to 100 favorites?) When I saw this block in an old quilt block book, it rang all my little bells. Half-triangle squares ... a lot of them. The design is a little bit ocean wave and a little bit pinwheel. There are options for different color palettes and secondary designs, so it is perfect for scraps.

The color palette for my quilt came about accidentally. I had pulled fabrics for three different projects: a stack of red, navy and yellow. When I saw them next to each other on the cutting table, it was a 'why didn't I think of that?' moment.

One last thing, it's a quirk. I call these units half-triangle squares while most of the quilting world calls them half square triangles. Whatever you choose to call them, make sure to get triangle paper to make them."

Carrie

"Other than having to make a thousand pinwheels, I absolutely loved seeing this quilt evolve from a stack of beachy prints, to triangles, to pinwheels and finally to this unique Pirouette block. To me, these delicate triangles feel like hundreds of pieces of sea glass, sunshine and sand on a pale blue ocean! It makes me dream of summer just by looking at this quilt. I can't wait to see it on the northern California coastline next summer!"

Joanna

Pirouette Block

8 ½" x 8 ½" unfinished

Eight at a Time HST Method Cutting Instructions:

Description		Cutting
Background	A	2 - 5 ¾" squares
	B	2 - 2 ½" x 4 ½" rectangles
	C	2 - 2 ½" squares
Half Square Triangle	D	2 - 5 ¾" squares

Cake Mix HST Method Cutting Instructions:

Description		Cutting
Background	A	1 - 10" square
	B	2 - 2 ½" x 4 ½" rectangles
	C	2 - 2 ½" squares
Half Square Triangle	D	1 - 10" square
Cake Mix Recipe #3 (CM3)		1 - Recipe Card

Triangles on a Roll HST Method Cutting Instructions:

Description		Cutting
Background	A	1 - 6 ¼" x 21" rectangle
	B	2 - 2 ½" x 4 ½" rectangles
	C	2 - 2 ½" squares
Half Square Triangle	D	1 - 6 ¼" x 21" rectangle
2" Finished Half-Square Triangle Paper (H200)		1 - two by six section (12 squares)

HST = Half Square Triangle

Piecing Instructions:

Since there are so many half square triangles in this block, I would recommend using either the Eight at a Time, Cake Mix or Triangles on a Roll method. Pick your favorite method and have fun!

Eight at a Time HST Method:

Draw two diagonal lines on the wrong side of the Fabric A squares.

With right sides facing, layer a Fabric A square with a Fabric D square.

Stitch ¼" from each side of the drawn lines.

Cut the unit into quarters and on the drawn lines.

Half Square Triangle Unit should measure 2 ½" x 2 ½".

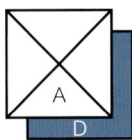 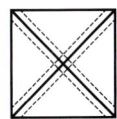 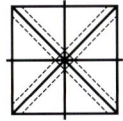

Make sixteen.

Cake Mix HST Method:

With right sides facing, layer the Fabric A square with the Fabric D square.

Follow instructions on the Cake Mix pad.

Half Square Triangle Unit should measure 2 ½" x 2 ½".

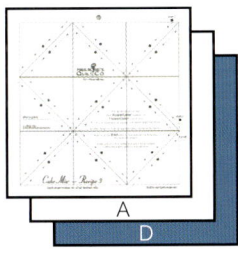

Make eighteen.

Triangles on a Roll HST Method:

With right sides facing, layer the Fabric A rectangle with the Fabric D rectangle.

Place the two by six section of 2" Finished Half-Square Triangle Paper on top and pin in place.

Set stitch length to 1.5 and sew on the dotted lines.

Cut apart on the solid lines.

Half Square Triangle Unit should measure 2 ½" x 2 ½".

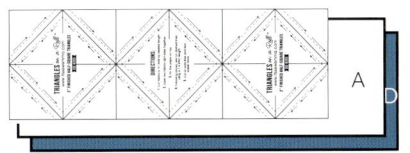

Make twenty-four.

Assemble Block. Press open.

Pirouette Block should measure 8 ½" x 8 ½".

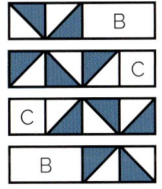 

Make one.
You will not use all Half Square Triangle Units.

Carrie's Pirouette Quilt

71 ½" x 71 ½"

Designed and Sewn by: Carrie Nelson / Quilted by: Carrie Straka (Instagram: @redvelvet_quilts)

Fabric Requirements:

Eight at a Time HST Method:	Cake Mix HST Method:	Triangles on a Roll HST Method:
3 yards - Background and Border	**3 yards - Background and Border**	**3 yards - Background and Border**

24 - 2 ½" x WOF strips, subcut into:
  128 - 2 ½" x 4 ½" rectangles   A
  128 - 2 ½" squares   B
	24 - 2 ½" x WOF strips, subcut into:
	  128 - 2 ½" x 4 ½" rectangles A
	  128 - 2 ½" squares B
		24 - 2 ½" x WOF strips, subcut into:
		  128 - 2 ½" x 4 ½" rectangles A
		  128 - 2 ½" squares B

16 - 1 ¼" x WOF strips, subcut into:
  64 - 1 ¼" x 8 ½" rectangles   C
	16 - 1 ¼" x WOF strips, subcut into:
	  64 - 1 ¼" x 8 ½" rectangles C
		16 - 1 ¼" x WOF strips, subcut into:
		  64 - 1 ¼" x 8 ½" rectangles C

8 - 2 ½" x WOF strips, sew end to end and subcut into:
  2 - 2 ½" x 67 ½" strips   D1
  2 - 2 ½" x 71 ½" strips   D2
	8 - 2 ½" x WOF strips, sew end to end and subcut into:
	  2 - 2 ½" x 67 ½" strips D1
	  2 - 2 ½" x 71 ½" strips D2
		8 - 2 ½" x WOF strips, sew end to end and subcut into:
		  2 - 2 ½" x 67 ½" strips D1
		  2 - 2 ½" x 71 ½" strips D2

20 Light Fat Quarters - Blocks	**36 Light Layer Cake squares - Blocks**	**27 Light Fat Eighths - Blocks**

From each 18" x 21" rectangle cut:
  4 - 5 ¾" squares (80 total)   E
	36 - 10" squares E	From each 9" x 21" rectangle cut:
		  1 - 6 ¼" x 21" strip (27 total) E

14 Yellow Fat Eighths - Blocks	**12 Yellow Layer Cake squares - Blocks**	**9 Yellow Fat Eighths - Blocks**

From each 9" x 21" rectangle cut:
  2 - 5 ¾" squares (28 total)   F
	12 - 10" squares F	From each 9" x 21" rectangle cut:
		  1 - 6 ¼" x 21" strip (9 total) F

12 Blue Fat Eighths - Blocks	**12 Blue Layer Cake squares - Blocks**	**9 Blue Fat Eighths - Blocks**

From each 9" x 21" rectangle cut:
  2 - 5 ¾" squares (24 total)   F
	12 - 10" squares F	From each 9" x 21" rectangle cut:
		  1 - 6 ¼" x 21" strip (9 total) F

14 Red Fat Eighths - Blocks	**12 Red Layer Cake squares - Blocks**	**9 Red Fat Eighths - Blocks**

From each 9" x 21" rectangle cut:
  2 - 5 ¾" squares (28 total)   F
	12 - 10" squares F	From each 9" x 21" rectangle cut:
		  1 - 6 ¼" x 21" strip (9 total) F

16 Red Scraps - Cornerstones	**16 Red Scraps - Cornerstones**	**16 Red Scraps - Cornerstones**

From each scrap cut:
  1 - 1 ¼" square (16 total)   G
	From each scrap cut:
	  1 - 1 ¼" square (16 total) G
		From each scrap cut:
		  1 - 1 ¼" square (16 total) G

Four ¼ yards - Binding	**Four ¼ yards - Binding**	**Four ¼ yards - Binding**

From each ¼ yard cut:
  2 - 2 ¼" x WOF strips (8 total)   H
	From each ¼ yard cut:
	  2 - 2 ¼" x WOF strips (8 total) H
		From each ¼ yard cut:
		  2 - 2 ¼" x WOF strips (8 total) H

	One Cake Mix Recipe Pad #3	One roll of 2" Half Square Triangle Paper by Triangles on a Roll
	36 - Recipe Cards	27 - two by six sections (12 squares each)
4 ⅝ yards - Backing	**4 ⅝ yards - Backing**	**4 ⅝ yards - Backing**

Carrie's Pirouette Quilt

Pirouette Blocks:

Since there are so many half square triangles in this block, I would recommend using either the Eight at a Time, Cake Mix or Triangles on a Roll method. Pick your favorite method and have fun!

Fabric placement is intended to be scrappy.

Eight at a Time HST Method:

Draw two diagonal lines on the wrong side of the Fabric E squares.

With right sides facing, layer a Fabric E square with a Fabric F square.

Stitch ¼" from each side of the drawn lines.

Cut the unit into quarters and on the drawn lines.

Half Square Triangle Unit should measure 2 ½" x 2 ½".

 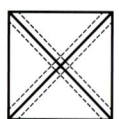 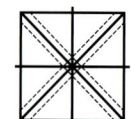

Make six hundred forty.

Cake Mix HST Method:

With right sides facing, layer a Fabric E square with a Fabric F square.

Follow instructions on the Cake Mix pad.

Half Square Triangle Unit should measure 2 ½" x 2 ½".

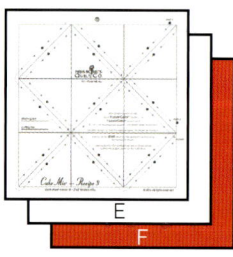

Make six hundred forty-eight.

Triangles on a Roll HST Method:

With right sides facing, layer a Fabric E strip with a Fabric F strip.

Place a two by six section of 2" Finished Half-Square Triangle Paper on top and pin in place.

Set stitch length to 1.5 and sew on the dotted lines.

Cut apart on the solid lines.

Half Square Triangle Unit should measure 2 ½" x 2 ½".

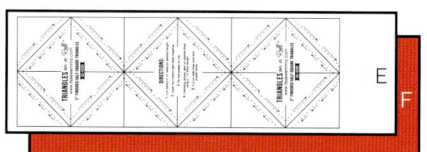

Make six hundred forty-eight.

Assemble Unit. Press open.

Pirouette Unit should measure 8 ½" x 8 ½".

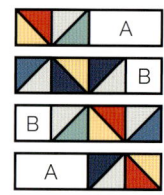 

Make sixty-four.
You may not use all Half Square Triangle Units.

Assemble Block. Press open.

Pirouette Block should measure 17 ¼" x 17 ¼".

Make sixteen.

Carrie's Pirouette Quilt

Quilt Center:

Assemble Quilt Center. Press open.

Quilt Center should measure 67 ½" x 67 ½".

Border:

Attach side borders using the Fabric D1 strips.

Attach top and bottom borders using the Fabric D2 strips.

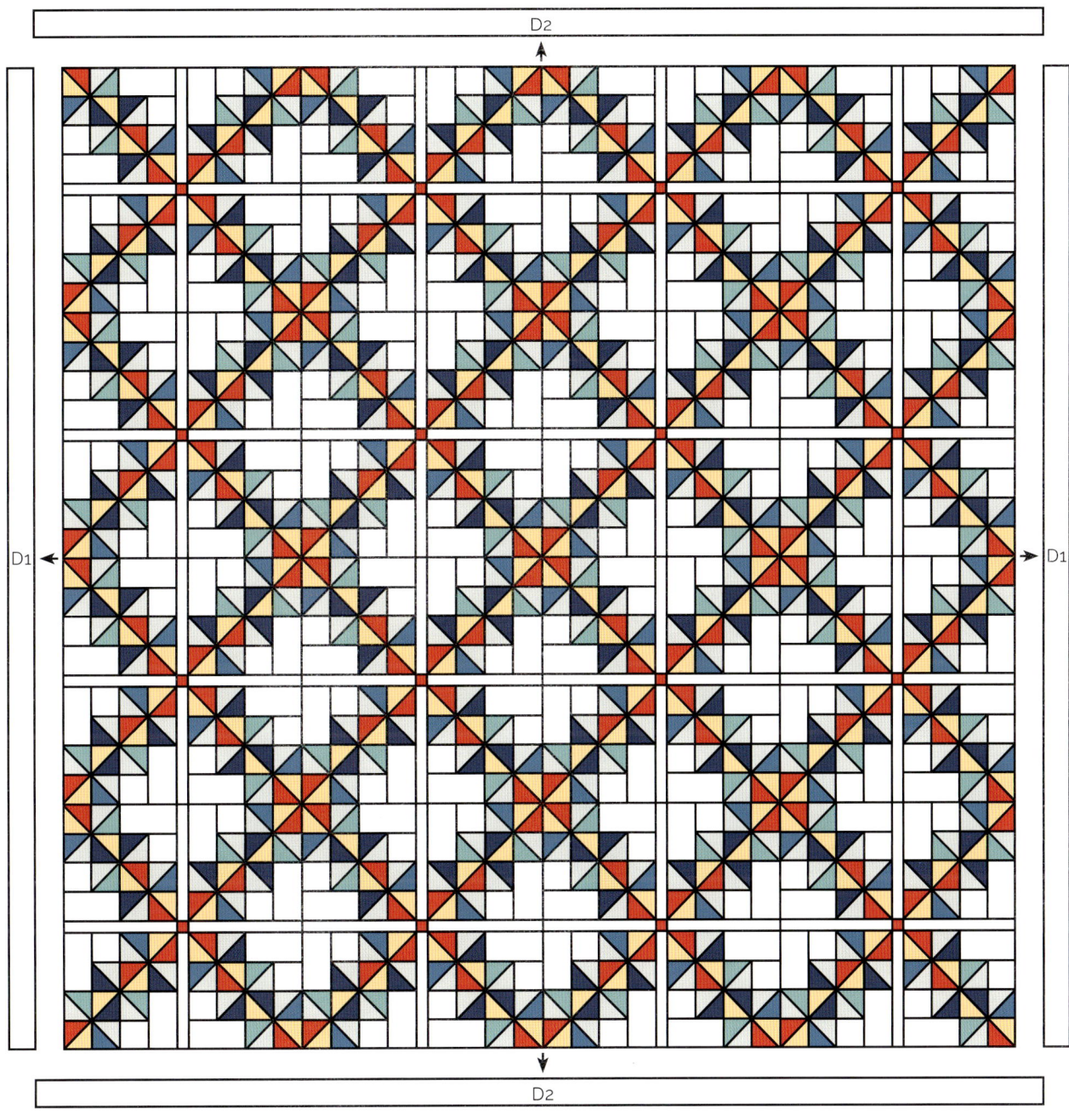

Finishing:

Piece the Fabric H strips end to end to make the scrappy binding. Press open for less bulk.
You will need approximately 316 inches for binding.

Quilt as desired.

Joanna's Pirouette Quilt

71 ½" x 71 ½"

Designed by: Joanna Figueroa / Sewn by: Cynthia Bird (Instagram: @cynthia.bird) and Megan Edgerton
Quilted by: Marion Bott (Instagram: @bottmarion)

Fabric Requirements:

Eight at a Time HST Method:	Cake Mix HST Method:	Triangles on a Roll HST Method:
3 yards - Background and Border	**3 yards - Background and Border**	**3 yards - Background and Border**

24 - 2 ½" x WOF strips, subcut into:
  128 - 2 ½" x 4 ½" rectangles A
  128 - 2 ½" squares B
	24 - 2 ½" x WOF strips, subcut into:
	  128 - 2 ½" x 4 ½" rectangles A
	  128 - 2 ½" squares B
		24 - 2 ½" x WOF strips, subcut into:
		  128 - 2 ½" x 4 ½" rectangles A
		  128 - 2 ½" squares B

16 - 1 ¼" x WOF strips, subcut into:
  64 - 1 ¼" x 8 ½" rectangles C
	16 - 1 ¼" x WOF strips, subcut into:
	  64 - 1 ¼" x 8 ½" rectangles C
		16 - 1 ¼" x WOF strips, subcut into:
		  64 - 1 ¼" x 8 ½" rectangles C

8 - 2 ½" x WOF strips, sew end to end and subcut into:
  2 - 2 ½" x 67 ½" strips D1
  2 - 2 ½" x 71 ½" strips D2
	8 - 2 ½" x WOF strips, sew end to end and subcut into:
	  2 - 2 ½" x 67 ½" strips D1
	  2 - 2 ½" x 71 ½" strips D2
		8 - 2 ½" x WOF strips, sew end to end and subcut into:
		  2 - 2 ½" x 67 ½" strips D1
		  2 - 2 ½" x 71 ½" strips D2

2 ½ yards - Block Background and Cornerstones	**3 yards - Block Background and Cornerstones**	**2 ⅔ yards - Block Background and Cornerstones**

14 - 5 ¾" x WOF strips, subcut into:
  82 - 5 ¾" squares E
	10 - 10" x WOF strips, subcut into:
	  37 - 10" squares E
		14 - 6 ¼" x WOF strips, subcut into:
		  28 - 6 ¼" x 21" strips E

1 - 1 ¼" x WOF strip, subcut into:
  16 - 1 ¼" squares F
	1 - 1 ¼" x WOF strip, subcut into:
	  16 - 1 ¼" squares F
		1 - 1 ¼" x WOF strip, subcut into:
		  16 - 1 ¼" squares F

⅝ yard - Accent	**¾ yard - Accent**	**⅔ yard - Accent**

3 - 5 ¾" x WOF strips, subcut into:
  16 - 5 ¾" squares G
	2 - 10" x WOF strips, subcut into:
	  8 - 10" squares G
		3 - 6 ¼" x WOF strips, subcut into:
		  6 - 6 ¼" x 21" strips G

22 Pastel Fat Eighths - Blocks	**29 Pastel Layer Cake squares - Blocks**	**22 Pastel Fat Eighths - Blocks**

From each 9" x 21" rectangle cut:
  3 - 5 ¾" squares (66 total) H
	29 - 10" squares H	From each 9" x 21" rectangle cut:
		  1 - 6 ¼" x 21" strip (22 total) H

⅔ yard - Binding	**⅔ yard - Binding**	**⅔ yard - Binding**
8 - 2 ¼" x WOF strips I	8 - 2 ¼" x WOF strips I	8 - 2 ¼" x WOF strips I
	One Cake Mix Recipe Pad #3	One roll of 2" Half Square Triangle Paper by Triangles on a Roll
	37 - Recipe Cards	22 - two by six sections (12 squares each)
4 ⅝ yards - Backing	**4 ⅝ yards - Backing**	**4 ⅝ yards - Backing**

Joanna's Pirouette Quilt

Pirouette Blocks:

Since there are so many half square triangles in this block, I would recommend using either the Eight at a Time, Cake Mix or Triangles on a Roll method. Pick your favorite method and have fun!

Fabric placement is intended to be scrappy.

Eight at a Time HST Method:

Draw two diagonal lines on the wrong side of the Fabric E squares.

With right sides facing, layer a Fabric E square with a Fabric G square.

Stitch ¼" from each side of the drawn lines.

Cut the unit into quarters and on the drawn lines.

Accent Half Square Triangle Unit should measure 2 ½" x 2 ½".

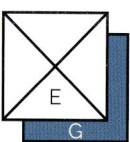 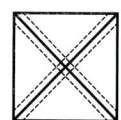 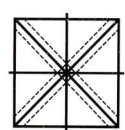

Make one hundred twenty-eight.

With right sides facing, layer a Fabric E square with a Fabric H square.

Stitch ¼" from each side of the drawn lines.

Cut the unit into quarters and on the drawn lines.

Multi Half Square Triangle Unit should measure 2 ½" x 2 ½".

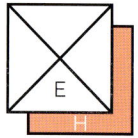 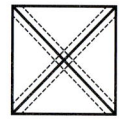 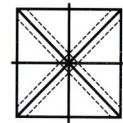

Make five hundred twenty-eight total.

Cake Mix HST Method:

With right sides facing, layer a Fabric E square with a Fabric G square.

Follow instructions on the Cake Mix pad.

Accent Half Square Triangle Unit should measure 2 ½" x 2 ½".

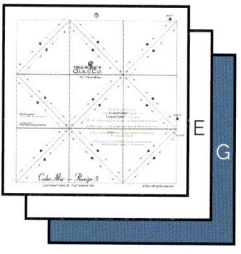

Make one hundred forty-four.

With right sides facing, layer a Fabric E square with a Fabric H square.

Follow instructions on the Cake Mix pad.

Multi Half Square Triangle Unit should measure 2 ½" x 2 ½".

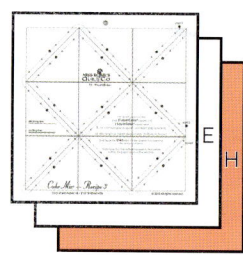

Make five hundred twenty-two total.

Triangles on a Roll HST Method:

With right sides facing, layer a Fabric E strip with a Fabric G strip.

Place a two by six section of 2" Finished Half-Square Triangle Paper on top and pin in place.

Set stitch length to 1.5 and sew on the dotted lines.

Cut apart on the solid lines.

Accent Half Square Triangle Unit should measure 2 ½" x 2 ½".

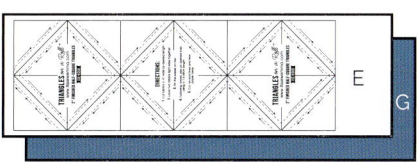

Make one hundred forty-four.

· ·

With right sides facing, layer a Fabric E strip with a Fabric H strip.

Place a two by six section of 2" Finished Half-Square Triangle Paper on top and pin in place.

Set stitch length to 1.5 and sew on the dotted lines.

Cut apart on the solid lines.

Multi Half Square Triangle Unit should measure 2 ½" x 2 ½".

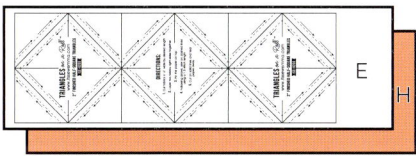

Make five hundred twenty-eight total.

· ·

Assemble Unit. Press open.

Pay close attention to Unit placement.

Pirouette Unit should measure 8 ½" x 8 ½".

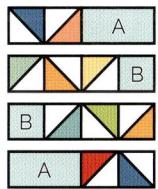 

Make sixty-four.
You will not use all Half Square Triangle Units.

Assemble Block. Press open.

Pirouette Block should measure 17 ¼" x 17 ¼".

Make sixteen.

Joanna's Pirouette Quilt

Quilt Center:

Assemble Quilt Center. Press open.

Quilt Center should measure 67 ½" x 67 ½".

Border:

Attach side borders using the Fabric D1 strips.

Attach top and bottom borders using the Fabric D2 strips.

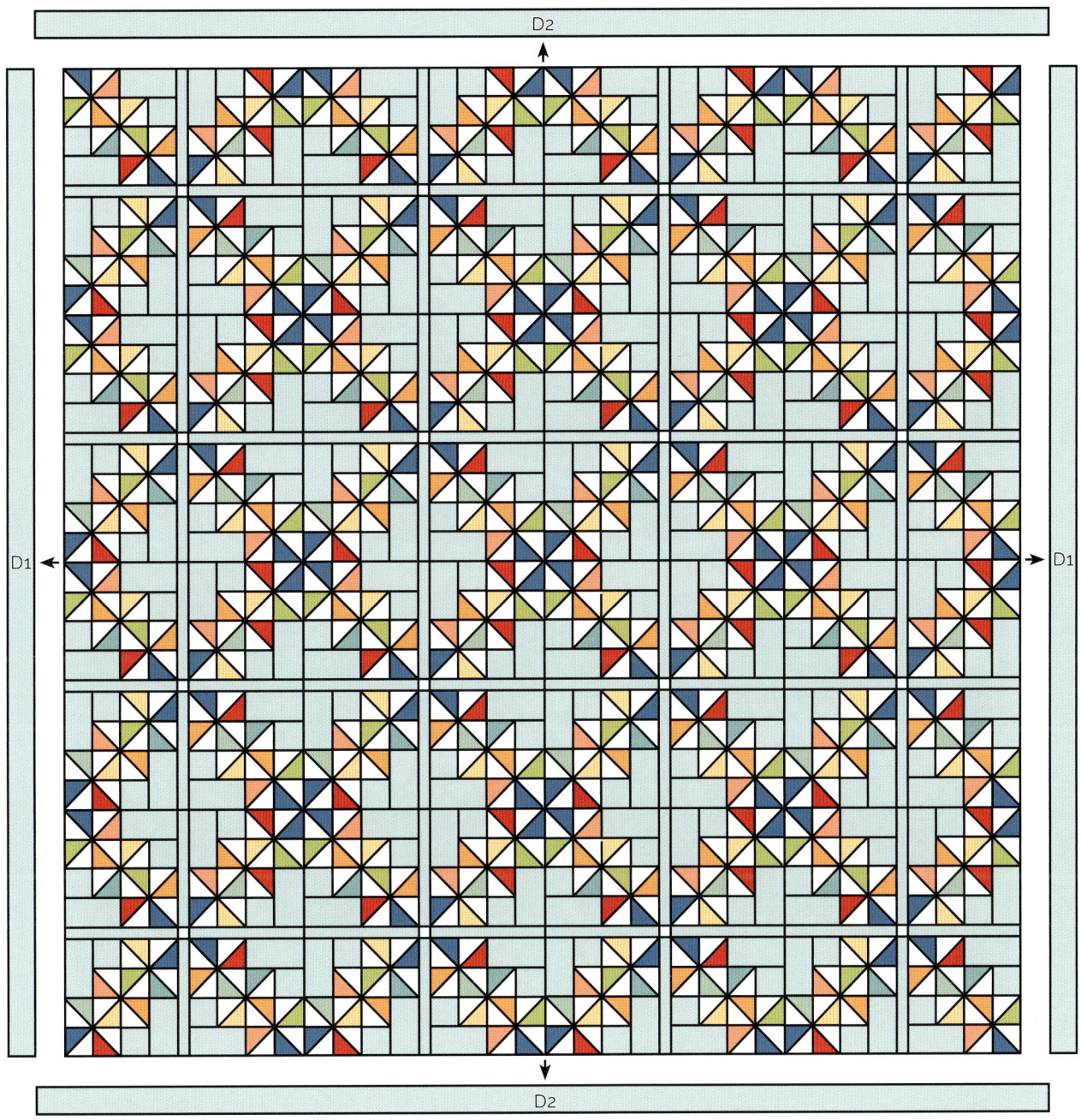

Finishing:

Piece the Fabric I strips end to end for binding.

Quilt and bind as desired.

Pirouette Tabletopper

24 ½" x 24 ½"

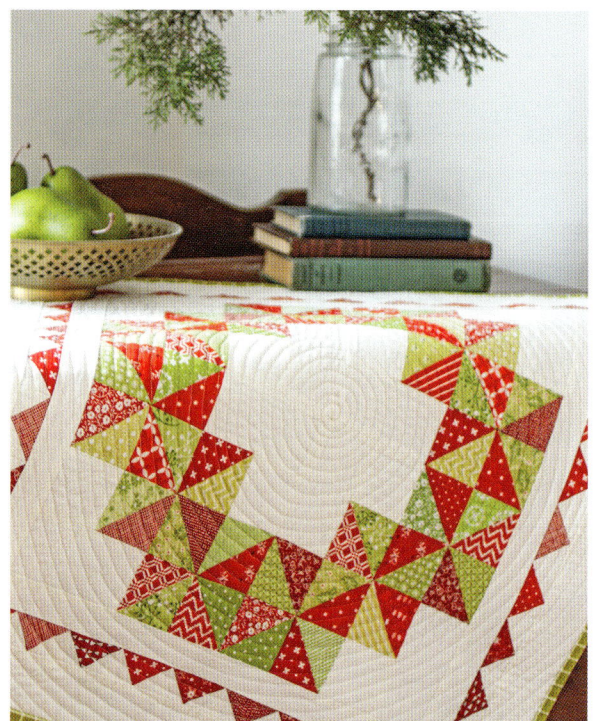

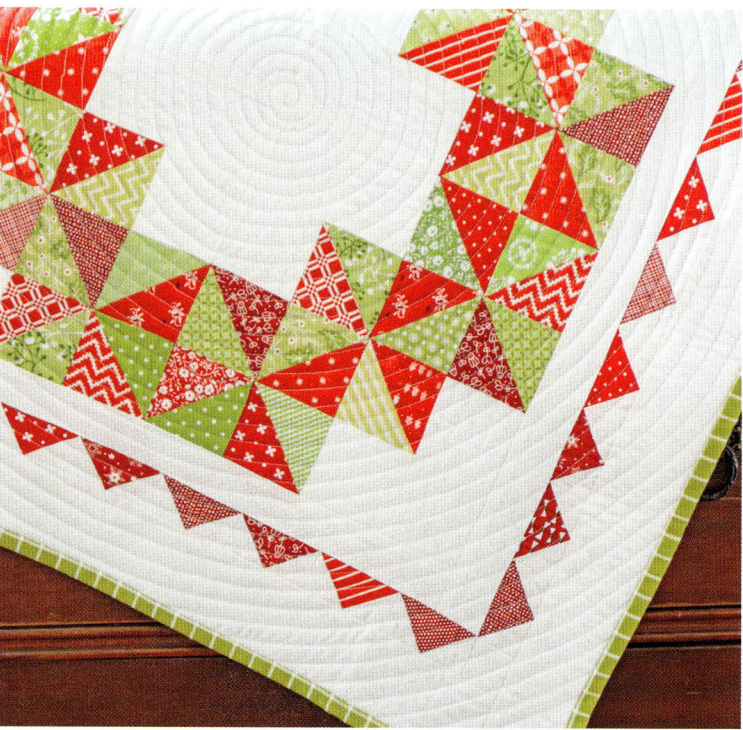

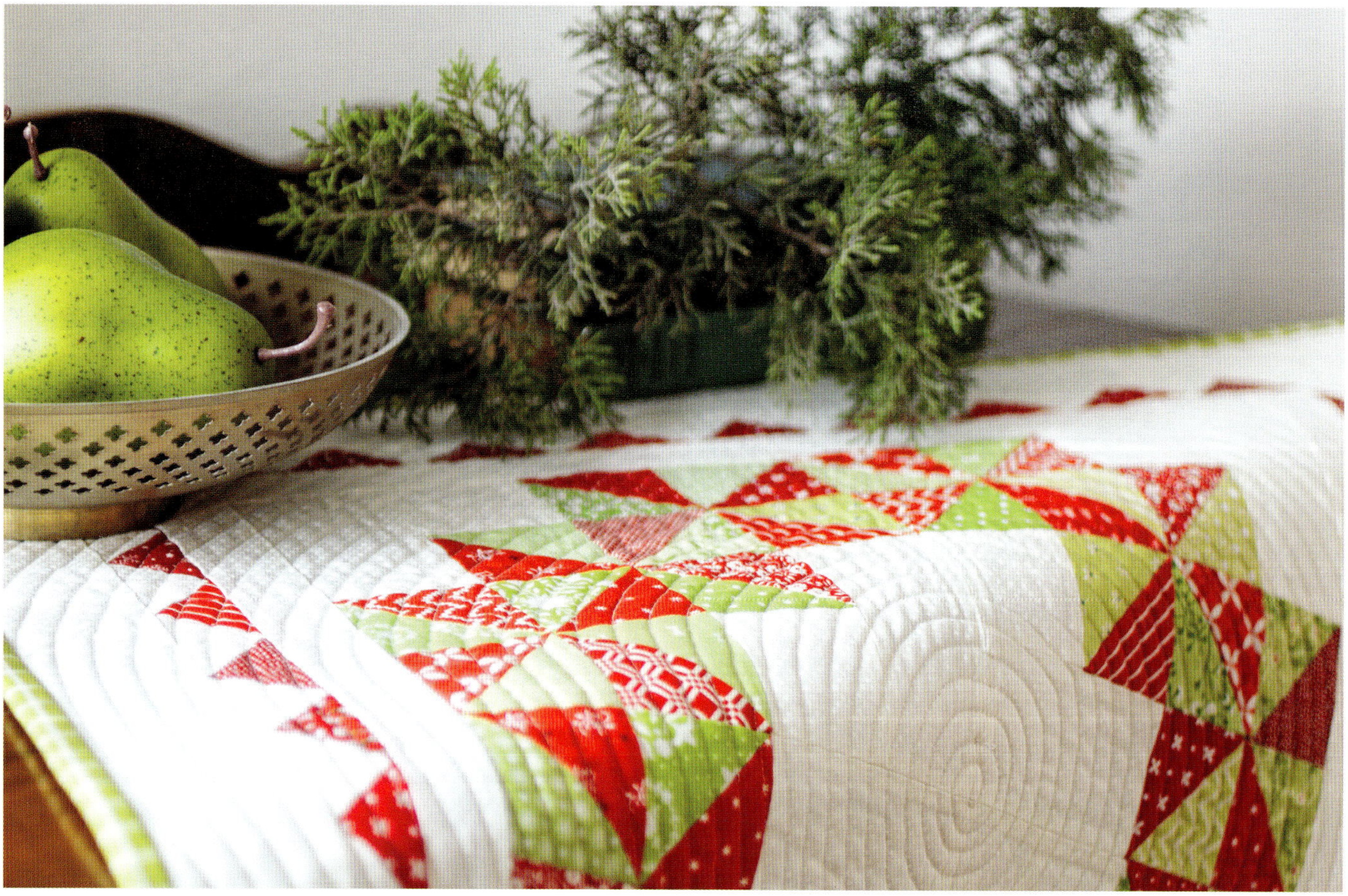

Designed by: Carrie Nelson / Sewn by: Melissa Corry (Instagram: @happyquiltingmc)

Fabric Requirements:

⅞ yard - Background and Border	
2 - 2 ½" x WOF strips, subcut into:	
8 - 2 ½" x 4 ½" rectangles	A
8 - 2 ½" squares	B
5 - 1 ½" x WOF strips, subcut into:	
2 - 1 ½" x 16 ½" rectangles .	C1
2 - 1 ½" x 18 ½" rectangles	C2
4 - 1 ½" squares	D
80 - 1 ½" squares	E
4 - 2 ½" x WOF strips, subcut into:	
2 - 2 ½" x 20 ½" strips	F1
2 - 2 ½" x 24 ½" strips	F2

20 Red Charm Pack squares - Blocks	
From each 5" square cut:	
1 - 3" square (20 total)	G
2 - 1 ½" x 2 ½" rectangles (40 total)	H

20 Green Charm Pack squares - Blocks	
From each 5" square cut:	
1 - 3" square (20 total)	I

⅓ yard - Binding	
3 - 2 ¼" x WOF strips	J

1 yard - Backing	

Meet Melissa Corry

Happy Quilting Melissa. How can you not be drawn to a blog and quilter with that name? After meeting years ago, Joanna and Carrie got to know Melissa as a wonderfully talented quilter, prolific author and pattern designer. As a mom to five kids, she didn't get to Quilt Market often, but it was always a treat to see her lovely, smiling face. Like Susan, she gets so much done, does she ever sleep?

Pirouette Blocks:

Draw a diagonal line on the wrong side of the Fabric I squares.

With right sides facing, layer a Fabric I square with a Fabric G square.

Stitch ¼" from each side of the drawn line.

Cut apart on the marked line.

TRIM Half Square Triangle Unit to measure 2 ½" x 2 ½".

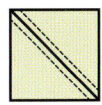 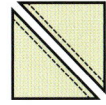

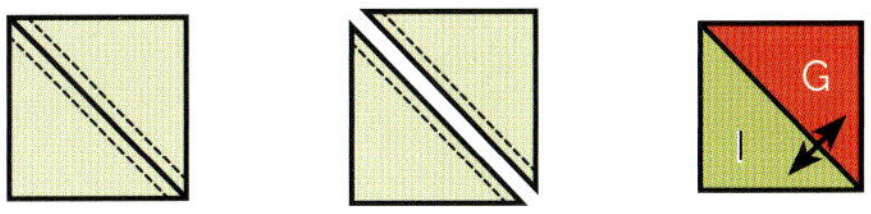

Make forty total.

. . . .

Assemble Block. Press open.
Pirouette Block should measure 8 ½" x 8 ½".

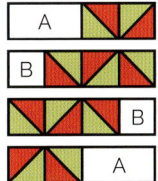 

Make four total.

. . . .

Tabletopper Center:

Assemble Tabletopper Center. Press open.
Tabletopper Center should measure 16 ½" x 16 ½".

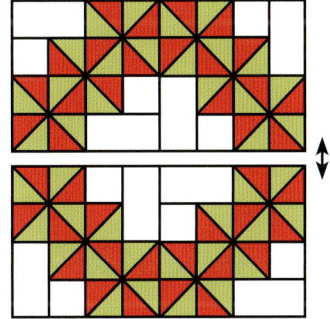

Pirouette Tabletopper

Border:

Attach side inner borders using the Fabric C1 rectangles.

Attach top and bottom inner borders using the Fabric C2 rectangles.

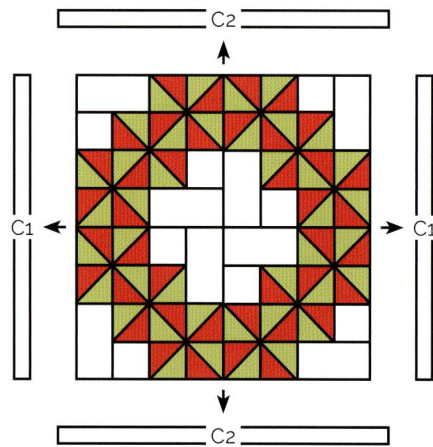

Draw a diagonal line on the wrong side of the Fabric E squares.

With right sides facing, layer a Fabric E square on one end of a Fabric H rectangle.

Stitch on the drawn line and trim ¼" away from the seam.

Repeat on the opposite end.

Flying Geese Unit should measure 1 ½" x 2 ½".

Make forty.

Assemble Border using nine Flying Geese Units.

Side Middle Border should measure 1 ½" x 18 ½".

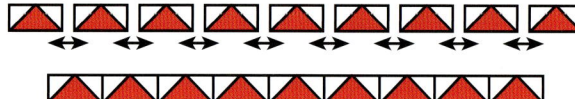

Make two.

« Joanna »

Over the years, I have tried many different half square triangle methods, and I know that people swear by so many different shortcuts and time-saving methods. Personally, I have settled on making them a bit larger and trimming them down to the perfect size. I don't often like to add in another step that might be unnecessary, but in this case I find that I love the results enough to do it.

« Carrie »

Like Joanna, I have tried many different methods to make half square triangles. Trimming to size is my go-to method, especially when I want a lot of variety. But I will use other methods when it will save time, or if I need a lot of matching half square triangles. For the Pirouette quilt, I used 2" Half Square Triangle Paper by Triangles on a Roll (#H200). Triangle paper is a great way to make a lot of identical half square triangles fast!

Assemble Border using two Fabric D squares and nine Flying Geese Units.

Top and Bottom Middle Border should measure 1 ½" x 20 ½".

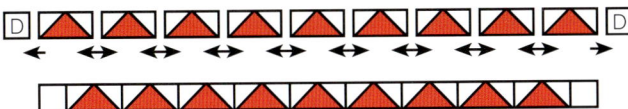

Make two.
You will not use all Flying Geese Units.

Attach the Side Middle Borders. Attach the Top and Bottom Middle Borders.

Attach side outer borders using the Fabric F1 strips. Attach top and bottom outer borders using the Fabric F2 strips.

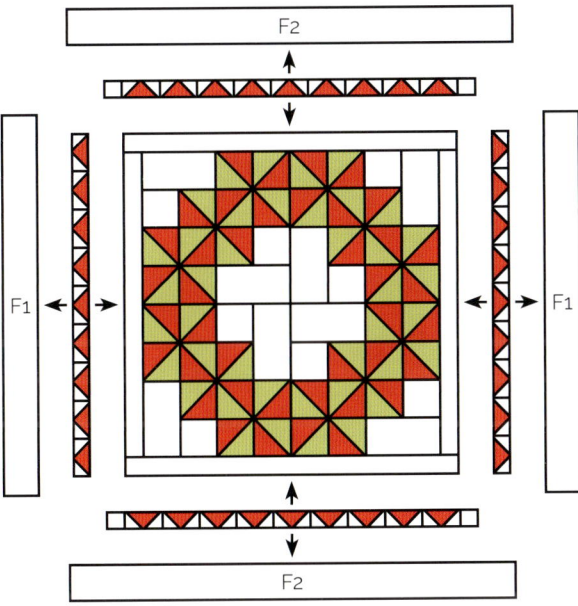

Finishing:

Piece the Fabric J strips end to end for binding.
Quilt and bind as desired.

Joanna's Pirouette Pillow

20" x 20"

Designed by: Joanna Figueroa
Sewn and Quilted by: Susan Vaughan
(Instagram: @thefeltedpear)

We have pillow finishing instructions and tips on page 14!

Fabric Requirements:

⅝ yard - Background	
5 - 3" x WOF strips, subcut into: 50 - 3" squares	A
2 Layer Cake squares - Blocks	
From each 10" square cut: 5 - 3" squares (10 total)	B
4 Layer Cake squares - Blocks	
From each 10" square cut: 4 - 3" squares (16 total)	C
4 Layer Cake squares - Blocks	
From each 10" square cut: 3 - 3" squares (12 total)	D
4 Layer Cake squares - Blocks	
From each 10" square cut: 2 - 3" squares (8 total)	E
4 Layer Cake squares - Blocks	
From each 10" square cut: 1 - 3" square (4 total)	F

Half Square Triangle Units:

Draw a diagonal line on the wrong side of the Fabric A squares.

With right sides facing, layer a Fabric A square with a Fabric B square.

Stitch ¼" from each side of the drawn line.

Cut apart on the marked line.

TRIM Half Square Triangle Unit One to measure 2 ½" x 2 ½".

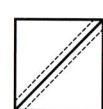 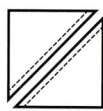

Make twenty total.

With right sides facing, layer a Fabric A square with a Fabric C square.

Stitch ¼" from each side of the drawn line.

Cut apart on the marked line.

TRIM Half Square Triangle Unit Two to measure 2 ½" x 2 ½".

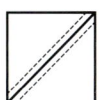 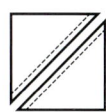

Make thirty-two total.

With right sides facing, layer a Fabric A square with a Fabric D square.

Stitch ¼" from each side of the drawn line.

Cut apart on the marked line.

TRIM Half Square Triangle Unit Three to measure 2 ½" x 2 ½".

 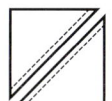

Make twenty-four total.

With right sides facing, layer a Fabric A square with a Fabric E square.

Stitch ¼" from each side of the drawn line.

Cut apart on the marked line.

TRIM Half Square Triangle Unit Four to measure 2 ½" x 2 ½".

 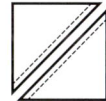 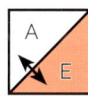

Make sixteen total.

With right sides facing, layer a Fabric A square with a Fabric F square.

Stitch ¼" from each side of the drawn line.

Cut apart on the marked line.

TRIM Half Square Triangle Unit Five to measure 2 ½" x 2 ½".

 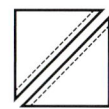

Make eight total.

Assemble Block. Press open.

Pirouette Block should measure 10 ½" x 10 ½".

Make four.

Pillow Center - Layout 1:

Assemble Pillow Center. Press open.

Pillow Center should measure 20 ½" x 20 ½".

Pillow Center - Layout 2:

Assemble Pillow Center. Press open.

Pillow Center should measure 20 ½" x 20 ½".

Carrie's Pirouette Pillow

20" x 20"

Designed, Sewn and Quilted by: Carrie Nelson

We have pillow finishing instructions and tips on page 14!

Fabric Requirements:

½ yard - Background and Border	
2 - 2 ½" x WOF strips, subcut into:	
8 - 2 ½" x 4 ½" rectangles	A
8 - 2 ½" squares	B
1 - 1 ½" x WOF strip, subcut into:	
4 - 1 ½" x 8 ½" rectangles	C
2 - 2" x WOF strips, subcut into:	
2 - 2" x 20 ½" strips	D
2 - 2" x 17 ½" strips	E
80 scraps - Blocks	
From 40 scraps cut:	
1 - 2 ½" square (40 total)	F
From 40 scraps cut:	
1 - 2 ½" square (40 total)	G
Scrap - Cornerstone	
From the scrap cut:	
1 - 1 ½" square	H

Pirouette Blocks:

Draw a diagonal line on the wrong side of the Fabric F squares.

With right sides facing, layer a Fabric F square with a Fabric G square.

Stitch on the drawn line and trim ¼" away from the seam.

Half Square Triangle Unit should measure 2 ½" x 2 ½".

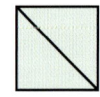 

Make forty total.

Assemble Block. Press open.
Pirouette Block should measure 8 ½" x 8 ½".

Make four total.

Pillow Center:

Assemble Pillow Center. Press toward the sashing.
Pillow Center should measure 17 ½" x 17 ½".

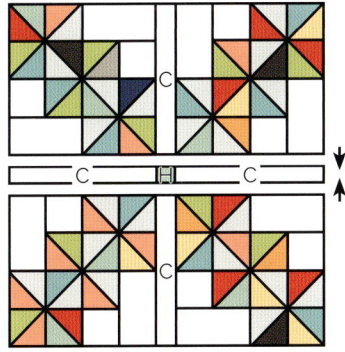

Border:

Attach side borders using the Fabric E strips.
Attach top and bottom borders using the Fabric D strips.

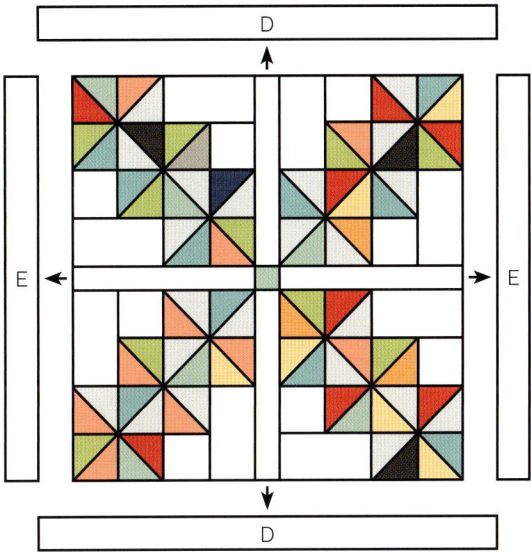

Pirouette Wreath Pillow

20" x 20"

Designed, Sewn and Quilted by: Carrie Nelson

We have pillow finishing instructions and tips on page 14!

Fabric Requirements:

½ yard - Background and Border	
2 - 2 ½" x WOF strips, subcut into:	
8 - 2 ½" x 4 ½" rectangles	A
8 - 2 ½" squares	B
2 - 2 ½" x WOF strips, subcut into:	
2 - 2 ½" x 20 ½" strips	C
2 - 2 ½" x 16 ½" strips	D

80 scraps - Blocks	
From 40 scraps cut:	
1 - 2 ½" square (40 total)	E
From 40 scraps cut:	
1 - 2 ½" square (40 total)	F

Pirouette Blocks:

Draw a diagonal line on the wrong side of the Fabric E squares.

With right sides facing, layer a Fabric E square with a Fabric F square.

Stitch on the drawn line and trim ¼" away from the seam.

Half Square Triangle Unit should measure 2 ½" x 2 ½".

Make forty total.

Assemble Block. Press open.
Pirouette Block should measure 8 ½" x 8 ½".

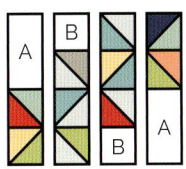 

Make four total.

Pillow Center:

Assemble Pillow Center. Press open.
Pillow Center should measure 16 ½" x 16 ½".

Border:

Attach side borders using the Fabric D strips
Attach top and bottom borders using the Fabric C strips.

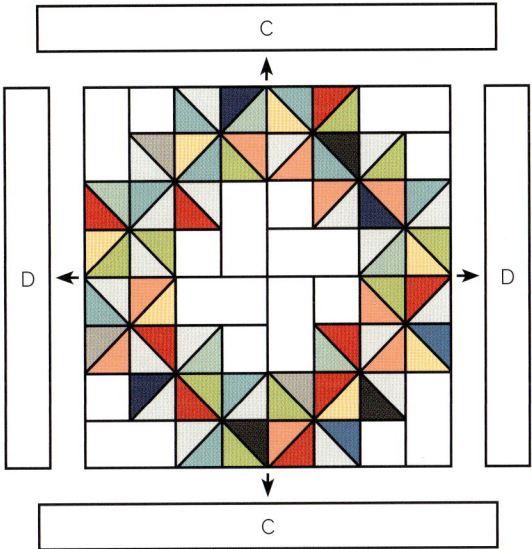

Pirouette Rectangle Pillow

16" x 20"

We have pillow finishing instructions and tips on page 14!

Fabric Requirements:

⅓ yard - Border	
1 - 4 ½" x WOF strip, subcut into:	
2 - 4 ½" x 20 ½" strips	A

80 scraps - Blocks	
From 40 scraps cut:	
1 - 2 ½" square (40 total)	B
From 40 scraps cut:	
1 - 2 ½" square (40 total)	C

Pillow Center:

Draw a diagonal line on the wrong side of the Fabric B squares.

With right sides facing, layer a Fabric B square with a Fabric C square.

Stitch on the drawn line and trim ¼" away from the seam.

Half Square Triangle Unit should measure 2 ½" x 2 ½".

Make forty total.

Assemble Pillow Center.

Pillow Center should measure 16 ½" x 20 ½".

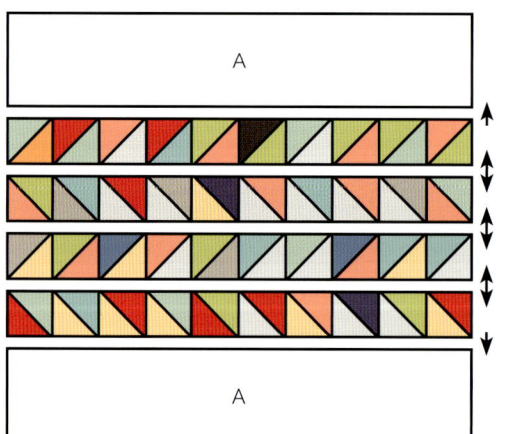

Pirouette Pinwheel Pincushion

3" x 6"

Designed by: Joanna Figueroa
Sewn and Quilted by: Cynthia Bird
(Instagram: @cynthia.bird)

We have pincushion finishing instructions and tips on page 12!

Fabric Requirements:

1 Layer Cake square - Background and Border	
From the 10" square cut:	
6 - 2" squares	A
2 - 1" x 6 ½" rectangles	B
3 Charm Pack squares - Blocks	
From each 5" square cut:	
2 - 2" squares (6 total)	C
6 Charm Pack squares - Pieced Backing	
From each 5" square cut:	
1 - 1 ½" x 3 ½" rectangle (6 total)	D
Scraps - Batting	
2 - 4" x 7" rectangles	

Pinwheel Block:

Draw a diagonal line on the wrong side of the Fabric A squares.

With right sides facing, layer a Fabric A square with a Fabric C square.

Stitch ¼" from each side of the drawn line.

Cut apart on the marked line.

TRIM Half Square Triangle Unit to measure 1 ½" x 1 ½".

Make twelve total.

Assemble Block using matching fabric. Press open.
Pinwheel Block should measure 2 ½" x 2 ½".

Make three total.

Pincushion Center:

Assemble Pincushion Center. Press open.
Pincushion Center should measure 2 ½" x 6 ½".

Pieced Backing:

Assemble Pieced Backing. Press open.
Pieced Backing should measure 3 ½" x 6 ½".

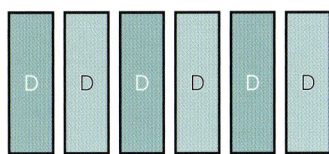

Border:

Attach top and bottom borders using the Fabric B
rectangles.

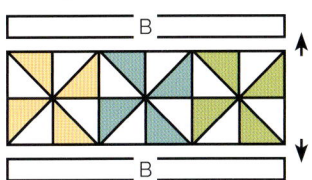

Pirouette Wreath Pincushion

5" x 5"

Designed, Sewn and Quilted by: Carrie Nelson

We have pincushion finishing instructions and tips on page 12!

Fabric Requirements:

1 Fat Eighth - Background and Border	
From the 9" x 21" rectangle cut:	
2 - 1" x 5 ½" rectangles	A
2 - 1" x 4 ½" rectangles	B
8 - 1" x 1 ½" rectangles	C
8 - 1" squares	D
5 Orange scraps - Blocks	
From each scrap cut:	
4 - 1 ½" squares (20 total)	E
5 Blue scraps - Blocks	
From each scrap cut:	
4 - 1 ½" squares (20 total)	F
1 Layer Cake square - Backing	
From the 10" square cut:	
1 - 6" square	
Scraps - Batting	
2 - 6" squares	

Pirouette Blocks:

Draw a diagonal line on the wrong side of the Fabric E squares.

With right sides facing, layer a Fabric E square with a Fabric F square.

Stitch ¼" from each side of the drawn line.

Cut apart on the marked line.

TRIM Half Square Triangle Unit to measure 1" x 1".

Make forty total.

Assemble Block. Press open.
Pirouette Block should measure 2 ½" x 2 ½".

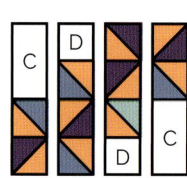 

Make four total.

Pincushion Center:

Assemble Pincushion Center. Press open.
Pincushion Center should measure 4 ½" x 4 ½".

"I used some leftover triangles from the Stitch & Flip method in the Oregon Trail Block to make this pincushion."

Carrie

Border:

Attach side borders using the Fabric B rectangles
Attach top and bottom borders using the Fabric A rectangles.

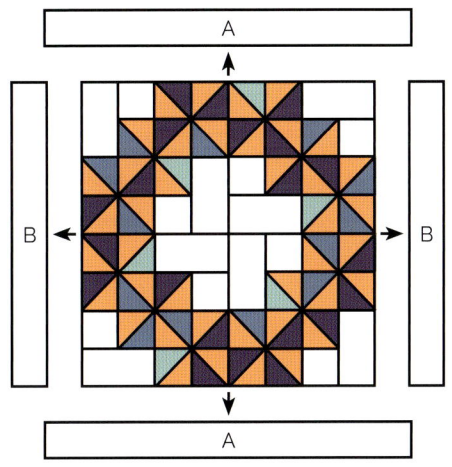

Pirouette Rectangle Pincushion

3" x 6"

Designed, Sewn and Quilted by: Carrie Nelson

We have pincushion finishing instructions and tips on page 12!

Fabric Requirements:

1 Layer Cake square - Background	
From the 10" square cut: 8 - 2" squares	A
8 scraps - Blocks	
From each scrap cut: 1 - 2" square (8 total)	B
1 Layer Cake square - Backing	
From the 10" square cut: 1 - 4" x 7" rectangle	
Scraps - Batting	
2 - 4" x 7" rectangles	

Pincushion Center:

Draw a diagonal line on the wrong side of the Fabric A squares.

With right sides facing, layer a Fabric A square with a Fabric B square.

Stitch on the drawn line and trim ¼" away from the seam.

Half Square Triangle Unit should measure 2" x 2".

Make eight total.

Assemble Pincushion Center. Press open.

Pincushion Center should measure 3 ½" x 6 ½".

Pirouette Hourglass Pincushion

4" x 4"

Designed, Sewn and Quilted by: Carrie Nelson

We have pincushion finishing instructions and tips on page 12!

Fabric Requirements:

1 Layer Cake square - Background	
From the 10" square cut: 8 - 2 ½" squares	A
8 scraps - Blocks	
From each scrap cut: 1 - 2 ½" square (8 total)	B
1 Charm Pack square - Backing	
1 - 5" square	
Scraps - Batting	
2 - 5" squares	

Hourglass Blocks:

Cut the Fabric A squares and Fabric B squares on the diagonal twice.

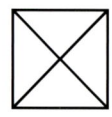 

Make thirty-two.

Make four from each scrap.
Make thirty-two total.

Assemble Block. Press open.
TRIM Hourglass Block to measure 1 ½" x 1 ½".

Make sixteen.

"I used some leftover triangles from the Stitch & Flip method in the House Blocks to make this pincushion."

Carrie

Pincushion Center:

Assemble Pincushion Center. Press open.
Pincushion Center should measure 4 ½" x 4 ½".

Chapter 5: Cathedral Garden

by Joanna Figueroa

"There are some blocks that I look at and admire from afar but don't feel drawn to make due to their style, complexity or the technique itself. That is how I always felt about traditional Cathedral Window blocks, until one day when I looked at them in a new way. In fact, the block didn't have to be made the traditional way ... I could piece it and still get the same feel and design of the original block without all of that fuss. It doesn't seem to matter what size these are, they still give you that great Cathedral Window feel without the traditional method."

Joanna

"Can I tell you a secret? While I am awestruck by the handwork that goes into making traditional Cathedral Window quilts, they were never my thing. But when I saw the drawing for this quilt, I was struck by the cool geometry of Joanna's variation. I also liked the versatility of the design. It will work with any style of fabric and color palette. I love that a stack of assorted low volume Layer Cake squares leftover from other projects could be so perfect. It turns out Cathedral Windows are my thing after all."

Carrie

Cathedral Garden Block

Small - 7" x 7" unfinished
Large - 8 ½" x 8 ½" unfinished

Small Block Cutting Instructions:

Description		Cutting
Background	A	4 - 3 ½" squares
Print	B	8 - 2 ½" squares
	C	1 - 1" x 7" rectangle
	D	2 - 1" x 3 ½" rectangles

Large Block Cutting Instructions:

Description		Cutting
Background	A	4 - 4" squares
Print	B	8 - 2 ¾" squares
	C	1 - 1 ½" x 8 ½" rectangle
	D	2 - 1 ½" x 4" rectangles

Piecing Instructions:

Draw a diagonal line on the wrong side of the Fabric B squares.

With right sides facing, layer Fabric B squares on opposite corners of a Fabric A square.

Stitch on the drawn lines and trim ¼" away from the seams.

Corner Unit should measure:

Small - 3 ½" x 3 ½"
Large - 4" x 4"

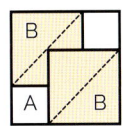 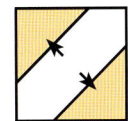

Make four.

Assemble Unit.

Cathedral Garden Unit should measure:

Small - 3 ½" x 7"
Large - 4" x 8 ½"

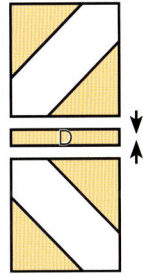 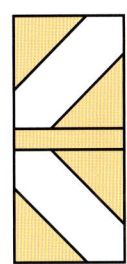

Make two.

Assemble Block.

Cathedral Garden Block should measure:

Small - 7" x 7"
Large - 8 ½" x 8 ½"

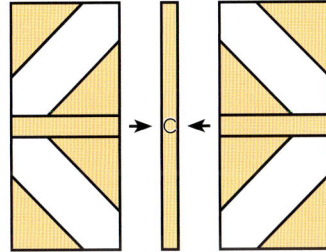 

Make one.

Off the Cuff ...
STARCHING

« Carrie »

I like to starch my fabrics before using them; this includes yardage and precuts. It serves two purposes for me. First, I get better results with starched fabric, especially on small pieces and blocks. Second, it serves to pre-shrink the fabric a bit, meaning I can use as much steam as I like when pressing. My process is to spray the fabric until it's almost saturated and let it air dry. Then I can press the fabric with steam.

I first learned to starch fabric years ago when we all still pre-washed our fabrics. Starching them made them "like new".

« Joanna »

This has not always been true for me, but now I also love to starch with Best Press or aerosol spray starch, but not to wetness, just dampness. Then I iron it dry. If it's a light colored fabric and I am concerned, even a little, I will use a damp cloth between the fabric and my iron. I do love the slightly crisp feeling of the fabric and the added control it gives me. I will ALWAYS starch woven, cross weave or lightweight fabrics. I will SOMETIMES starch standard quilting cottons, but not always. It is based on how small or difficult the pieces will be in the quilt. I will NEVER do it on precuts. I am way too worried about those suckers shrinking on me!

Joanna's Cathedral Garden Quilt

73 ½" x 81 ½"

Designed by: Joanna Figueroa / Sewn by: Joanna Figueroa and Susan Vaughan
(Instagram: @thefeltedpear) / Quilted by: Diana Johnson (Instagram: @quiltedgrammy)

Fabric Requirements:

24 Low Volume Fat Quarters - Blocks	
From each 18" x 21" rectangle cut: 12 - 3 ½" squares (288 total)	A

24 Print Fat Quarters - Blocks	
From each 18" x 21" rectangle cut: 24 - 2 ½" squares (576 total)	B
3 - 1" x 7" rectangles (72 total)	C
6 - 1" x 3 ½" rectangles (144 total)	D

2 ⅜ yards - Sashing and Border	
9 - 2 ½" x WOF strips, subcut into: 140 - 2 ½" squares	E
27 - 1 ½" x WOF strips, subcut into: 161 - 1 ½" x 7" rectangles	F
4 - 2" x WOF strips, sew end to end and subcut into: 2 - 2" x 69" strips	G
4 - 2 ¼" x WOF strips, sew end to end and subcut into: 2 - 2 ¼" x 64 ½" strips	H

⅓ yard - Cornerstones	
4 - 1 ½" x WOF strips, subcut into: 90 - 1 ½" squares	I

⅞ yard - Middle Border	
9 - 2 ½" x WOF strips, subcut into: 68 - 2 ½" x 4 ½" rectangles	J

1 yard - Outer Border	
9 - 3" x WOF strips, sew end to end and subcut into: 2 - 3" x 76 ½" strips	K1
2 - 3" x 73 ½" strips	K2

¾ yard - Binding	
9 - 2 ¼" x WOF strips	L

7 yards - Backing	

Refer to page 126 for Small Cathedral Garden Block instructions.

Small Cathedral Garden Blocks:

Assemble Block using matching fabric.
Small Cathedral Garden Block should measure 7" x 7".

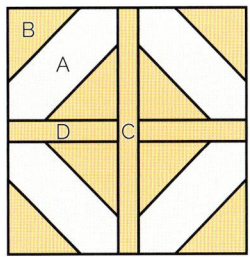

Make seventy-two total.

Joanna's Cathedral Garden Quilt

Quilt Center:

Assemble Quilt Center using Fabric F rectangles for sashing and Fabric I squares for cornerstones. Press toward the sashing.

Quilt Center should measure 61 ½" x 69".

Border:

Draw a diagonal line on the wrong side of 136 Fabric E squares.
With right sides facing, layer a marked Fabric E square on one end of a Fabric J rectangle.
Stitch on the drawn line and trim ¼" away from the seam.

Repeat on the opposite end.
Flying Geese Unit should measure 2 ½" x 4 ½".

Make sixty-eight.

Assemble Border using eighteen Flying Geese Units.
Side Middle Border should measure 2 ½" x 72 ½".

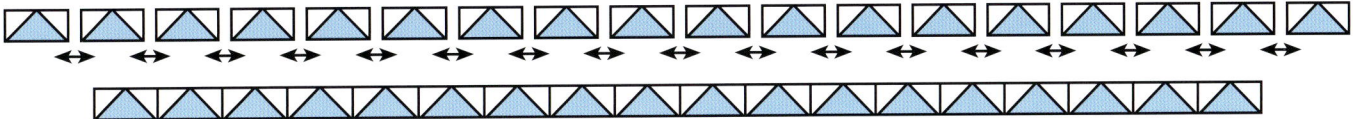

Make two.

Assemble Border using two Fabric E squares and sixteen Flying Geese Units.
Top and Bottom Middle Border should measure 2 ½" x 68 ½".

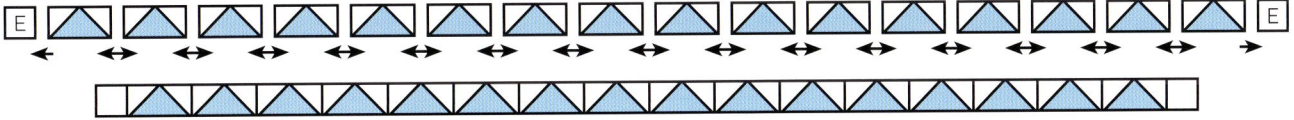

Make two.

Joanna's Cathedral Garden Quilt

Attach side inner borders using the Fabric G strips. Attach top and bottom inner borders using the Fabric H strips.

Attach the Side Middle Borders. Attach the Top and Bottom Middle Borders.

Attach side outer borders using the Fabric K1 strips. Attach top and bottom outer borders using the Fabric K2 strips.

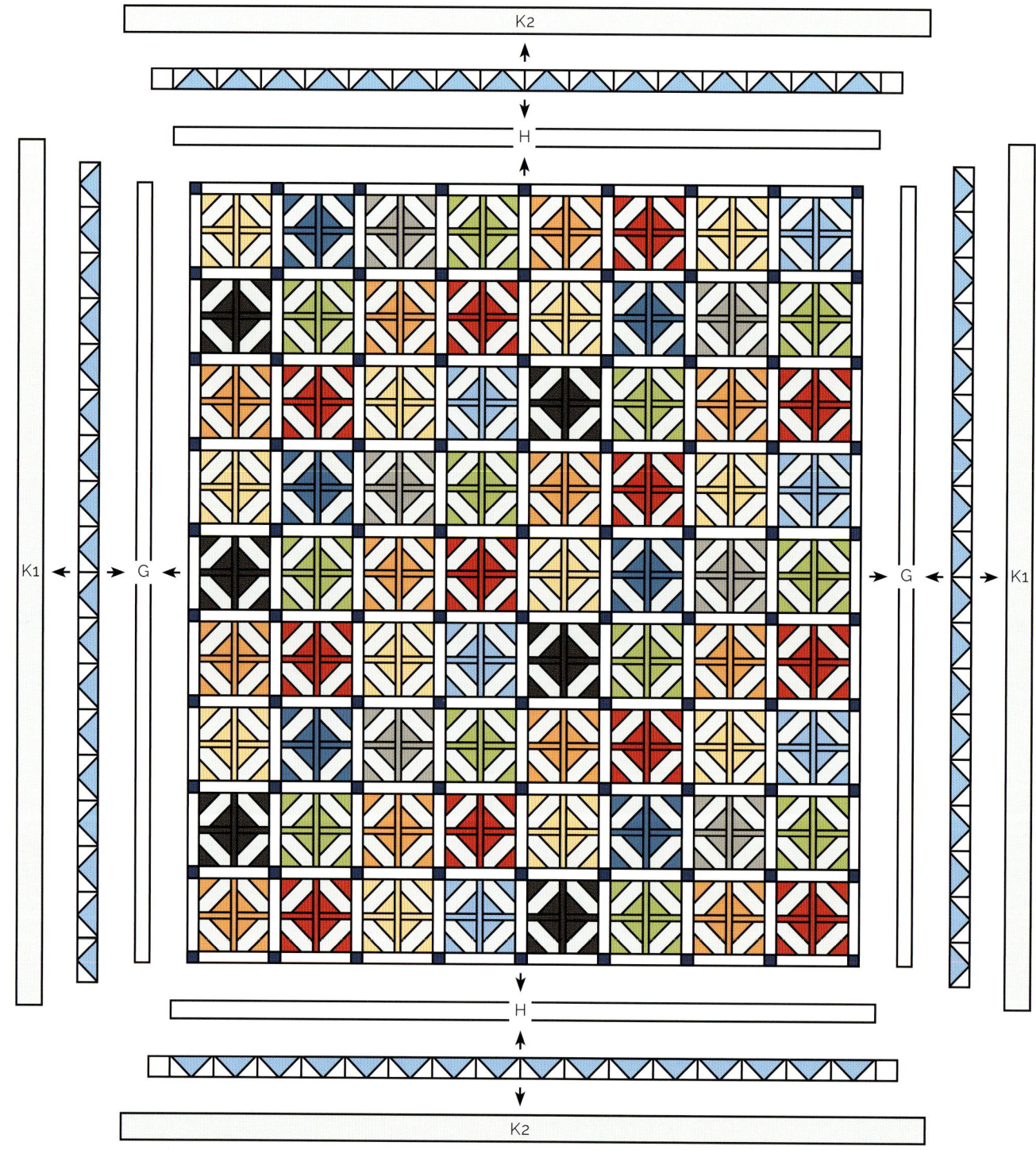

Finishing:

Piece the Fabric L strips end to end for binding.
Quilt and bind as desired.

Carrie's Cathedral Garden Quilt

68 ½" x 68 ½"

Designed by: Carrie Nelson / Sewn by: Judy Adams (Instagram: @jmaquilts)
Quilted by: Carrie Straka (Instagram: @redvelvet_quilts)

Fabric Requirements:

4 ⅓ yards - Background, Sashing and Border

22 - 3 ½" x WOF strips, subcut into: 256 - 3 ½" squares	A
9 - 2 ½" x WOF strips, subcut into: 132 - 2 ½" squares	B
24 - 1 ½" x WOF strips, subcut into: 144 - 1 ½" x 7" rectangles	C
7 - 2" x WOF strips, sew end to end and subcut into:	
2 - 2" x 61 ½" strips	D1
2 - 2" x 64 ½" strips	D2

22 Low Volume Fat Quarters* - Blocks, Cornerstones and Border

From each 18" x 21" rectangle cut:	
3 - 2 ½" x 4 ½" rectangles (66 total)	E
24 - 2 ½" squares (528 total)	F
4 - 1 ½" squares (88 total)	G
3 - 1" x 7" rectangles (66 total)	H
6 - 1" x 3 ½" rectangles (132 total)	I

⅔ yard - Binding

8 - 2 ¼" x WOF strips	J

4 ⅜ yards - Backing

* Low Volume Fat Quarter cutting:

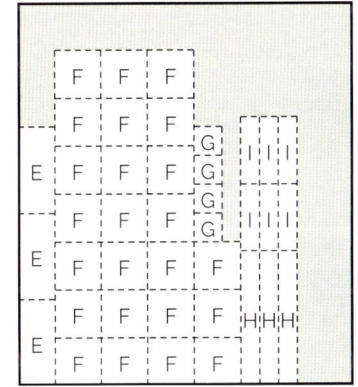

Refer to page 126 for Small Cathedral Garden Block instructions.

Small Cathedral Garden Blocks:

Assemble Block using matching fabric.

Small Cathedral Garden Block should measure 7" x 7".

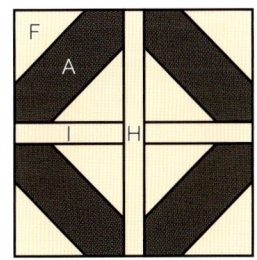

Make sixty-four total.

You will not use all Fabric F squares, Fabric H rectangles and Fabric I rectangles.

Carrie's Cathedral Garden Quilt

Quilt Center:

Assemble Quilt Center using Fabric C rectangles for sashing and Fabric G squares for cornerstones. Press toward the sashing.

Quilt Center should measure 61 ½" x 61 ½".

You will not use all Fabric G squares.

Border:

Draw a diagonal line on the wrong side of 128 Fabric B squares.

With right sides facing, layer a marked Fabric B square on one end of a Fabric E rectangle.

Stitch on the drawn line and trim ¼" away from the seam.

Repeat on the opposite end.

Flying Geese Unit should measure 2 ½" x 4 ½".

Make sixty-four.

You will not use all Fabric E rectangles.

"When I have leftover triangles from making Stitch & Flip corners, I save them to make pillows and pincushions!"

Carrie

Assemble Border using sixteen Flying Geese Units.

Side Outer Border should measure 2 ½" x 64 ½".

Make two.

Assemble Border using two Fabric B squares and sixteen Flying Geese Units.

Top and Bottom Outer Border should measure 2 ½" x 68 ½".

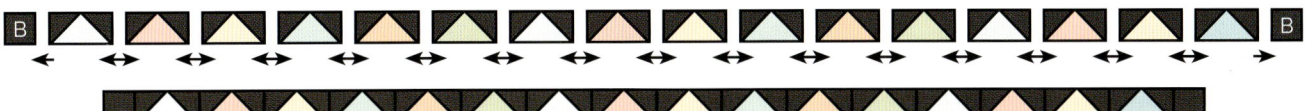

Make two.

Carrie's Cathedral Garden Quilt

Attach side inner borders using the Fabric D1 strips. Attach top and bottom inner borders using the Fabric D2 strips.

Attach the Side Outer Borders. Attach the Top and Bottom Outer Borders.

Finishing:

Piece the Fabric J strips end to end for binding.

Quilt and bind as desired.

Off the Cuff ...

BORDERS

« Joanna »

A couple of things I swear by on borders:

1. I never sew them together diagonally. I believe that it creates a more noticeable line, and I am not that worried about the straight seam.

2. I always piece them and never do length of fabric. There is no way I could ever justify all of that fabric waste, even if it looks better.

3. I always measure both sides three times to make sure that I have the number right. If my sides are different, I always take the average and cut both to the same measurement.

« Carrie »

I'm the opposite, I prefer a diagonal seam when piecing my border strips together.

Reading that Joanna also doesn't do length of fabric borders made me laugh because I don't like length of fabric either. It always seemed so wasteful. (Ironic given that both Joanna and I should be all for selling more yardage!) Being efficient with the fabric is one of the reasons I love pieced borders.

Measure. Measure. Measure. Agreed. Before measuring, I also give the sides of the quilt a good pressing as the handling during assembly can cause one or more sides to stretch a bit. I also check seam allowances to make sure I haven't "wandered off" at any of the ends.

Cathedral Garden Throw

49 ¾" x 59 ½"

Designed by: Joanna Figueroa / Sewn by: Susan Vaughan (Instagram: @thefeltedpear)
Quilted by: Sally Corona (Instagram: @coronaquiltworks)

Fabric Requirements:

1 ⅞ yards - Background and Sashing	
8 - 4" x WOF strips, subcut into:	
80 - 4" squares	A
13 - 2 ¼" x WOF strips, subcut into:	
49 - 2 ¼" x 8 ½" rectangles	B

20 Layer Cake squares* - Blocks	
From each 10" square cut:	
8 - 2 ¾" squares (160 total)	C
1 - 1 ½" x 8 ½" rectangle (20 total)	D
2 - 1 ½" x 4" rectangles (40 total)	E

1 Fat Quarter - Cornerstones	
From the 18" x 21" rectangle cut:	
30 - 2 ¼" squares	F

⅝ yard - Inner Border	
6 - 2 ¼" x WOF strips, sew end to end and subcut into:	
2 - 2 ¼" x 51" strips	G1
2 - 2 ¼" x 44 ¾" strips	G2

⅔ yard - Outer Border	
6 - 3" x WOF strips, sew end to end and subcut into:	
2 - 3" x 54 ½" strips	H1
2 - 3" x 49 ¾" strips	H2

⅝ yard - Binding	
7 - 2 ¼" x WOF strips	I

3 ⅓ yards - Backing	

* Layer Cake square cutting:

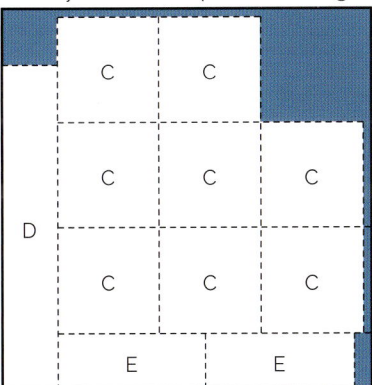

Refer to page 126 for Large Cathedral Garden Block instructions.

Large Cathedral Garden Blocks:

Assemble Block using matching fabric.
Large Cathedral Garden Block should measure 8 ½" x 8 ½".

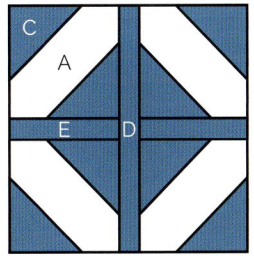

Make twenty total.

Cathedral Garden Throw

Quilt Center:

Assemble Quilt Center using Fabric B rectangles for sashing and Fabric F squares for cornerstones. Press toward the sashing.

Quilt Center should measure 41 ¼" x 51".

Meet Susan Vaughan

Susan is one of the sweetest, kindest quilter friends ever. She and Joanna met and immediately connected several years ago over their shared love of all things fig and pear, as well as quilting, of course. Susan now helps out with too many different Fig Tree things to count although she started in the industry with a "felt toys" business ... hence the name, The Felted Pear. She is also an editor extraordinaire and the mom of a beautiful crafter in the making, Sophie. Susan has contributed to the Moda Bakeshop for years and is always working on many projects at once.

Border:

Attach side inner borders using the Fabric G1 strips. Attach top and bottom inner borders using the Fabric G2 strips.

Attach side outer borders using the Fabric H1 strips. Attach top and bottom outer borders using the Fabric H2 strips.

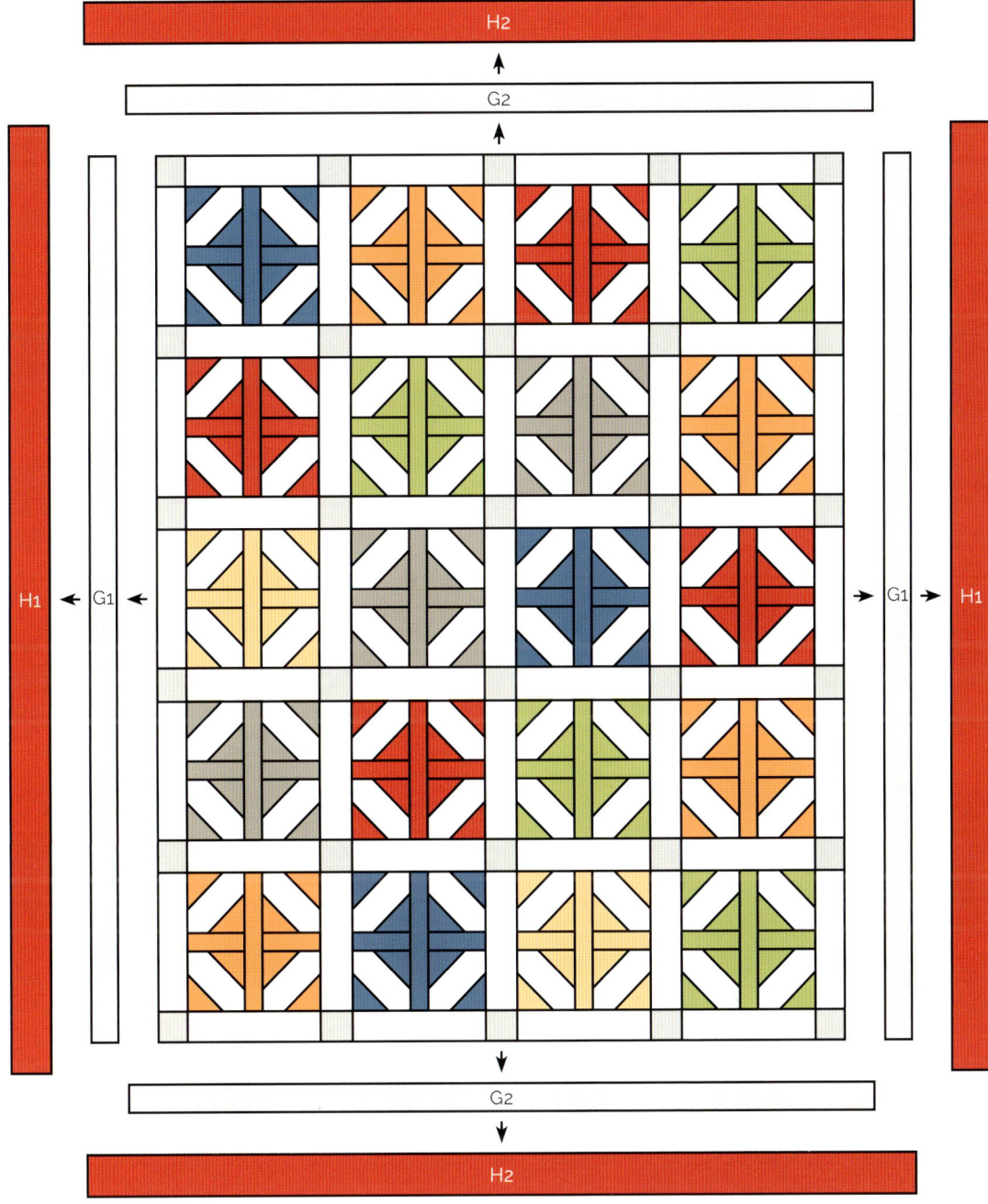

Finishing:

Piece the Fabric I strips end to end for binding.

Quilt and bind as desired.

Chapter 6:
Neighborhood

by Carrie Nelson

"I've tried to figure out what it is about house blocks and house quilts that I love so much. Every reason I can think of also applies to most other blocks. Is it because houses and neighborhoods convey a sense of home, of belonging somewhere? I wish I knew. I only know that they will always be some of my favorite quilts.

What I love about this quilt is that it captures the feel of my childhood neighborhood, where the houses were a mix of different styles and colors. Our white, Cape Cod-style home was next door to a sunny yellow saltbox."

Carrie

"It might have something to do with the fact that I was working on this quilt during the early fall months or perhaps because autumn is my absolute favorite time of the year, but I wanted to create the fall neighborhood of my dreams. Full of oranges, browns and plums ... my neighborhood would be Fig Tree Autumn epitomized! I am so incredibly excited to bring this one out next fall and feature it on the couch as my new favorite autumn throw!"

Joanna

Left House Block

10 ½" x 10 ½" unfinished

Cutting Instructions:

Background	A	2 - 3" squares
	B	1 - 1 ½" x 3 ½" rectangle
	C	2 - 1 ½" x 3" rectangles
Chimneys	D	2 - 1 ½" squares
House Front	E	2 - 2" x 7" rectangles
	F	2 - 1 ½" x 2 ½" rectangles
House Side	G	1 - 2" x 3 ½" rectangle
	H	2 - 1 ½" x 7" rectangles
	I	2 - 1 ½" x 3 ½" rectangles
	J	2 - 1 ½" x 2" rectangles
Roof Front	K	1 - 3" x 5 ½" rectangle
Roof Side	L	1 - 3" x 8" rectangle
Front Window	M	1 - 2" x 2 ½" rectangle
Side Windows	N	4 - 1 ½" x 2" rectangles
Door	O	1 - 2 ½" x 3 ½" rectangle

Piecing Instructions:

Assemble Unit.

Chimney Unit should measure 1 ½" x 10 ½".

Make one.

On the wrong side of the Fabric L rectangle, mark a dot 3" down from the top right corner. Draw a line from the top left corner to the dot.

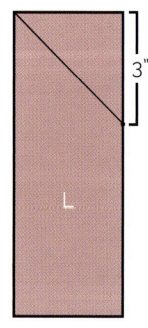

Make one.

With right sides facing, layer the Fabric L rectangle with the Fabric K rectangle. Stitch on the drawn line and trim ¼" away from the seam.

Partial Roof Unit should measure 3" x 10 ½".

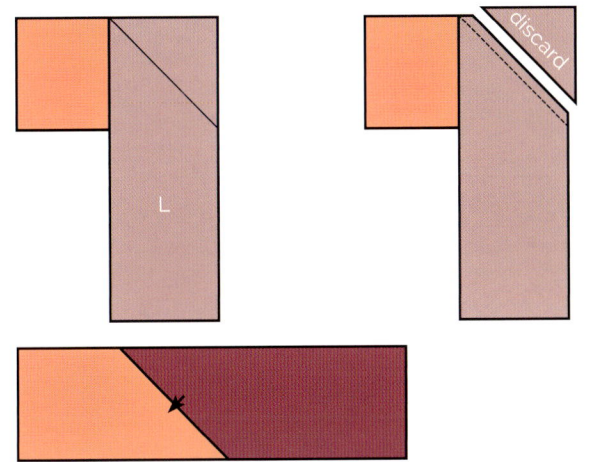

Make one.

Draw a diagonal line on the wrong side of the Fabric A squares.

With right sides facing, layer a Fabric A square on the left end of the Partial Roof Unit.

Stitch on the drawn line and trim ¼" away from the seam.

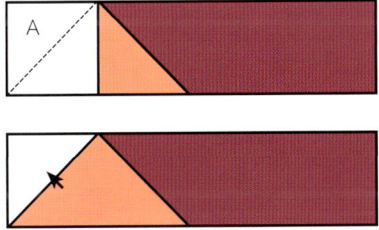

Repeat on the right end.

Roof Unit should measure 3" x 10 ½".

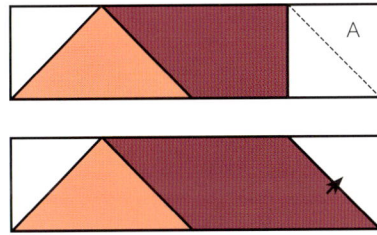

Make one.

Assemble Unit.

House Front Unit should measure 5 ½" x 7".

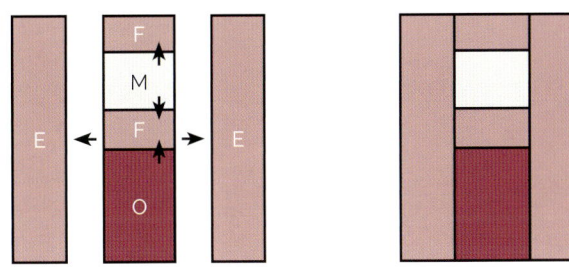

Make one.

Assemble Unit.

Partial House Side Unit should measure 3 ½" x 7".

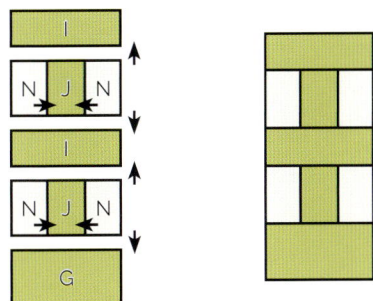

Make one.

Assemble Unit.

House Side Unit should measure 5 ½" x 7".

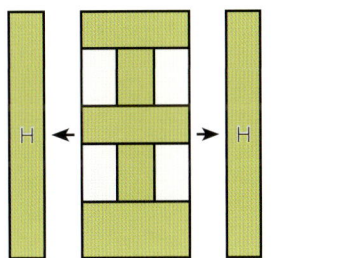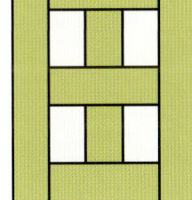

Make one.

Left House Block

Assemble Block.

Left House Block should measure 10 ½" x 10 ½".

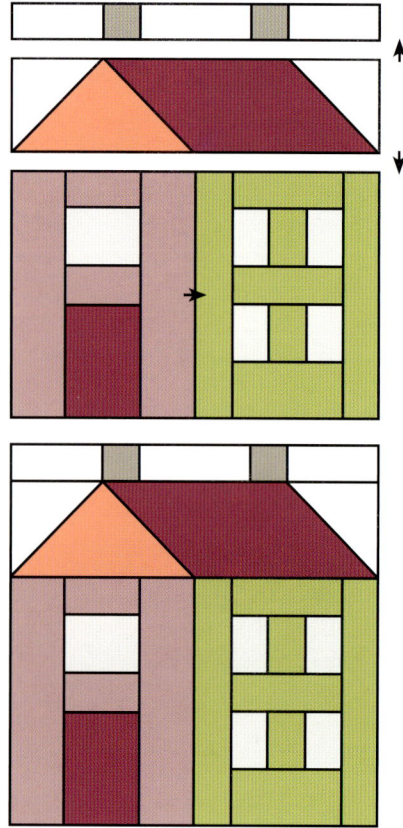

Make one.

« Joanna »

Here's another one of those simple tips that makes such a huge difference when piecing, in my opinion. Whenever you have a "point to catch", like on the tip of a star or the point of a flying geese, be sure that you are sewing it on the side of the point itself. As you approach the point, start to veer in or out a tiny bit to ensure that you catch it right at the point. Your block will forgive the slight veer, and you will have a perfect point each time!

« Carrie »

Huh? Points aren't supposed to be nicked off?

Two things to add here ... let's say you're making a quilt top with star blocks alternating with plain squares. When you're joining the rows, join only those sections with the star block on the top, stopping and starting at the seam junctions. Then flip the row and sew on the other side, stitching the blocks that weren't stitched the first time. (Does that make sense?) Second, when you want the best results possible and there are points on both sides, it's worth taking the time to stitch the seam with a longer stitch, six to eight stitches to the inch. Check the points, and if you're happy with the results, re-stitch the seam with a regular stitch length.

Right House Block

10 ½" x 10 ½" unfinished

Cutting Instructions:

Description		Cutting
Background	A	2 - 3" squares
	B	1 - 1 ½" x 3 ½" rectangle
	C	2 - 1 ½" x 3" rectangles
Chimneys	D	2 - 1 ½" squares
House Front	E	2 - 2" x 7" rectangles
	F	2 - 1 ½" x 2 ½" rectangles
House Side	G	1 - 2" x 3 ½" rectangle
	H	2 - 1 ½" x 7" rectangles
	I	2 - 1 ½" x 3 ½" rectangles
	J	2 - 1 ½" x 2" rectangles
Roof Front	K	1 - 3" x 5 ½" rectangle
Roof Side	L	1 - 3" x 8" rectangle
Front Window	M	1 - 2" x 2 ½" rectangle
Side Windows	N	4 - 1 ½" x 2" rectangles
Door	O	1 - 2 ½" x 3 ½" rectangle

Piecing Instructions:

Assemble Unit.

Chimney Unit should measure 1 ½" x 10 ½".

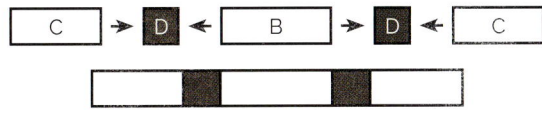

Make one.

On the wrong side of the Fabric L rectangle, mark a dot 3" down from the top left corner. Draw a line from the top right corner to the dot.

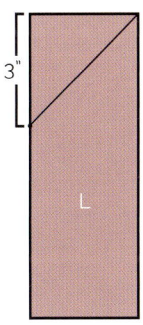

Make one.

Right House Block

With right sides facing, layer the Fabric L rectangle with the Fabric K rectangle. Stitch on the drawn line and trim ¼" away from the seam.

Partial Roof Unit should measure 3" x 10 ½".

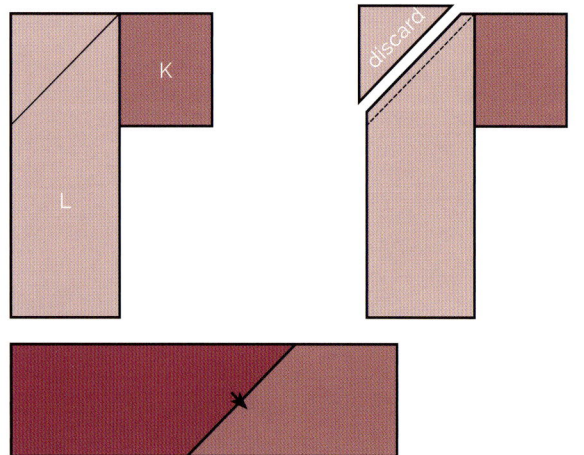

Make one.

Draw a diagonal line on the wrong side of the Fabric A squares.

With right sides facing, layer a Fabric A square on the left end of a Partial Roof Unit.

Stitch on the drawn line and trim ¼" away from the seam.

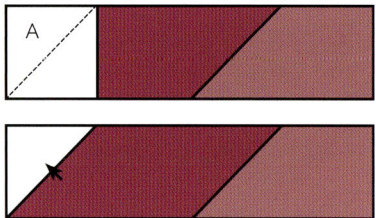

Repeat on the right end.

Roof Unit should measure 3" x 10 ½".

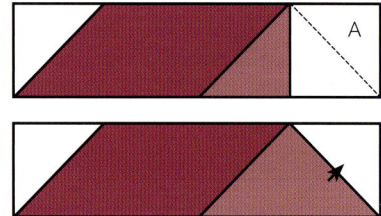

Make one.

Assemble Unit.

House Front Unit should measure 5 ½" x 7".

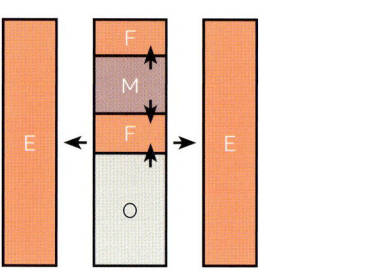 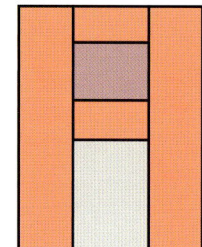

Make one.

Assemble Unit.

Partial House Side Unit should measure 3 ½" x 7".

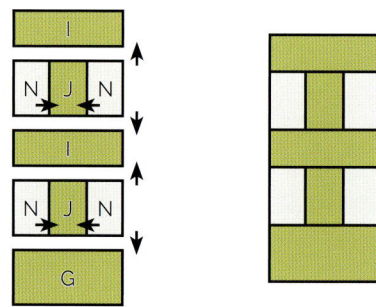

Make one.

Assemble Unit.

House Side Unit should measure 5 ½" x 7".

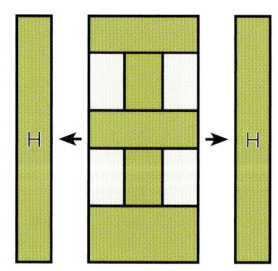 

Make one.

Assemble Block.

Right House Block should measure 10 ½" x 10 ½".

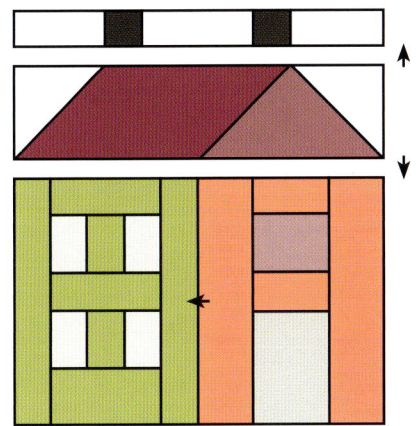 

Make one.

Tall Condo Block

5 ½" x 10 ½" unfinished

Piecing Instructions:

Draw a diagonal line on the wrong side of the Fabric A squares.

With right sides facing, layer a Fabric A square on one end of the Fabric B rectangle.

Stitch on the drawn line and trim ¼" away from the seam.

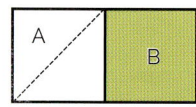
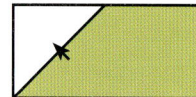

Repeat on the opposite end.

Condo Roof Unit should measure 3" x 5 ½".

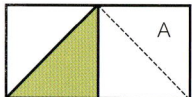
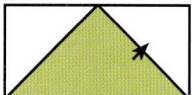

Make one.

Assemble Unit.

Partial Tall Condo Unit should measure 3 ½" x 8".

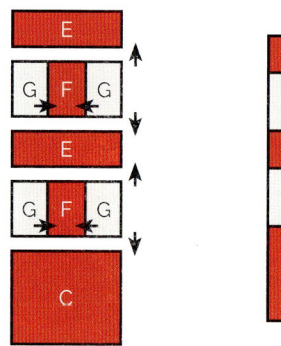

Make one.

Assemble Block.

Tall Condo Block should measure 5 ½" x 10 ½".

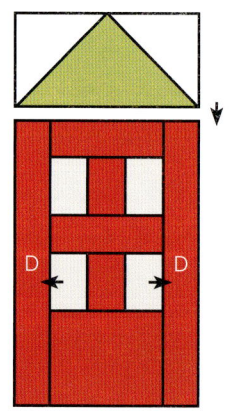
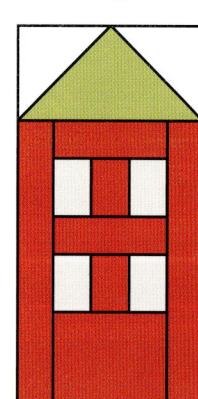

Make one.

Cutting Instructions:

Description		Cutting
Background	A	2 – 3" squares
Condo Roof	B	1 – 3" x 5 ½" rectangle
Tall Condo Front	C	1 – 3" x 3 ½" rectangle
	D	2 – 1 ½" x 8" rectangles
	E	2 – 1 ½" x 3 ½" rectangles
	F	2 – 1 ½" x 2" rectangles
Windows	G	4 – 1 ½" x 2" rectangles

Short Condo Block

5 ½" x 10 ½" unfinished

Piecing Instructions:

Draw a diagonal line on the wrong side of the Fabric A squares.

With right sides facing, layer a Fabric A square on one end of the Fabric C rectangle.

Stitch on the drawn line and trim ¼" away from the seam.

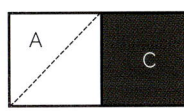 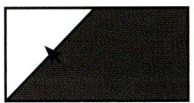

Repeat on the opposite end.

Condo Roof Unit should measure 3" x 5 ½".

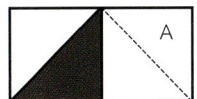 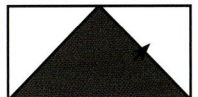

Make one.

Assemble Unit.

Partial Short Condo Unit should measure 3 ½" x 7".

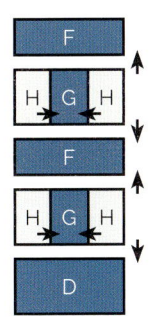 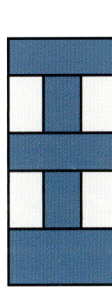

Make one.

Assemble Block.

Short Condo Block should measure 5 ½" x 10 ½".

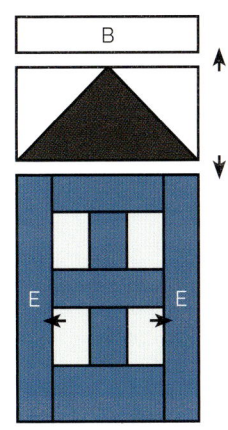 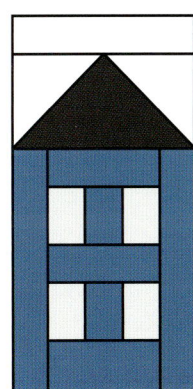

Make one.

Cutting Instructions:

Description		Cutting
Background	A	2 - 3" squares
	B	1 - 1 ½" x 5 ½" rectangle
Condo Roof	C	1 - 3" x 5 ½" rectangle
Short Condo Front	D	1 - 2" x 3 ½" rectangle
	E	2 - 1 ½" x 7" rectangles
	F	2 - 1 ½" x 3 ½" rectangles
	G	2 - 1 ½" x 2" rectangles
Windows	H	4 - 1 ½" x 2" rectangles

Carrie's Neighborhood Quilt

60 ½" x 64 ½"

Designed by Carrie Nelson / Sewn by: Thelma Childers (Instagram: @thelmacupcake)
Quilted by: Teresa Silva

Fabric Requirements:

1 ¾ yards - Background, Sashing and Border

5 - 3" x WOF strips, subcut into:	
58 - 3" squares	A
7 - 2 ½" x WOF strips, sew end to end and subcut into:	
4 - 2 ½" x 54 ½" strips	B
6 - 2" x 2 ½" rectangles	C
12 - 1 ½" x WOF strips, subcut into:	
8 - 1 ½" x 5 ½" rectangles	D
14 - 1 ½" x 3 ½" rectangles	E
28 - 1 ½" x 3" rectangles	F
25 - 1 ½" x 10 ½" rectangles	G
6 - 1 ¼" x WOF strips, subcut into:	
6 - 1 ¼" x 10 ½" rectangles	H
12 - 1 ¼" x 2 ½" rectangles	I
12 - 1 ¼" x 2" rectangles	J
48 - 1 ¼" squares	K

⅞ yard - Border

7 - 3 ½" x WOF strips, sew end to end and subcut into:	
2 - 3 ½" x 58 ½" strips	L1
2 - 3 ½" x 60 ½" strips	L2

6 Layer Cake squares - Chimneys & Tree Trunk

From each 10" square cut:	
6 - 1 ½" squares (36 total)	M
1 - 1 ¼" x 2 ½" rectangle (6 total)	N
1 - 1" x 2" rectangle (6 total)	O

14 Layer Cake squares - House Front

From each 10" square cut:	
2 - 2" x 7" rectangles (28 total)	P
2 - 1 ½" x 2 ½" rectangles (28 total)	Q

14 Layer Cake squares - House Side

From each 10" square cut:	
1 - 2" x 3 ½" rectangle (14 total)	R
2 - 1 ½" x 7" rectangles (28 total)	S
2 - 1 ½" x 3 ½" rectangles (28 total)	T
2 - 1 ½" x 2" rectangles (28 total)	U

5 Layer Cake squares - House Roof Front

From each 10" square cut:	
3 - 3" x 5 ½" rectangles (15 total)	V

5 Layer Cake squares - House Roof Side

From each 10" square cut:	
3 - 3" x 8" rectangles (15 total)	W

2 Layer Cake squares - House Door

From each 10" square cut:	
8 - 2 ½" x 3 ½" rectangles (16 total)	X

7 Layer Cake squares - Tall Condo Front

From each 10" square cut:	
1 - 3" x 3 ½" rectangle (7 total)	Y
2 - 1 ½" x 8" rectangles (14 total)	Z
2 - 1 ½" x 3 ½" rectangles (14 total)	AA
2 - 1 ½" x 2" rectangles (14 total)	BB

4 Layer Cake squares - Condo Roof

From each 10" square cut:	
4 - 3" x 5 ½" rectangles (16 total)	CC

8 Layer Cake squares - Short Condo Front

From each 10" square cut:	
1 - 2" x 3 ½" rectangle (8 total)	DD
2 - 1 ½" x 7" rectangles (16 total)	EE
2 - 1 ½" x 3 ½" rectangles (16 total)	FF
2 - 1 ½" x 2" rectangles (16 total)	GG

7 Layer Cake squares - House Front Window

From each 10" square cut:	
2 - 2" x 2 ½" rectangles (14 total)	HH

7 Layer Cake squares - House Side Windows

From each 10" square cut:	
8 - 1 ½" x 2" rectangles (56 total)	II

3 Layer Cake squares - Condo Windows

From each 10" square cut:	
20 - 1 ½" x 2" rectangles (60 total)	JJ

6 Layer Cake squares - Tree Top

From each 10" square cut:	
1 - 2 ¾" x 8 ½" rectangle (6 total)	KK
1 - 2 ½" x 7 ½" rectangle (6 total)	LL

⅝ yard - Binding

7 - 2 ¼" x WOF strips	MM

4 ¼ yards - Backing

Carrie's Neighborhood Quilt

House Blocks:

Refer to pages 146 to 151 for House Block instructions.

Each House Block uses eight coordinating prints.

Assemble Block using coordinating fabric.
Left House Block should measure 10 ½" x 10 ½".

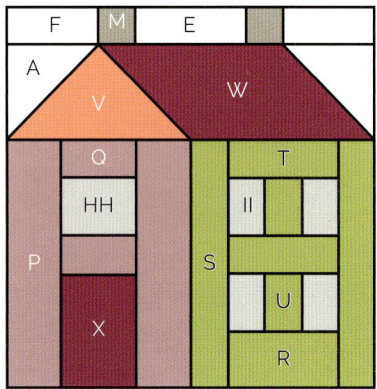

Make ten.

Assemble Block using coordinating fabric.
Right House Block should measure 10 ½" x 10 ½".

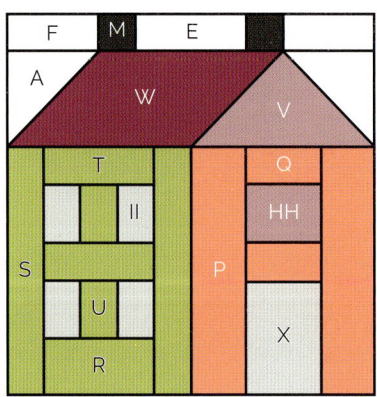

Make four.
You will not use all Fabric M squares, Fabric V rectangles, Fabric W rectangles and Fabric X rectangles.

Condo Blocks:

Refer to pages 152 to 153 for Condo Block instructions.

Each Condo Block uses three coordinating prints.

Assemble Block using coordinating fabric.
Tall Condo Block should measure 5 ½" x 10 ½".

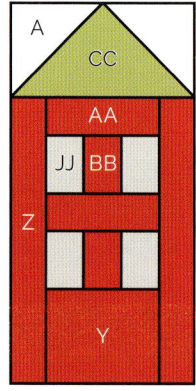

Make seven.

Assemble Block using coordinating fabric.
Short Condo Block should measure 5 ½" x 10 ½".

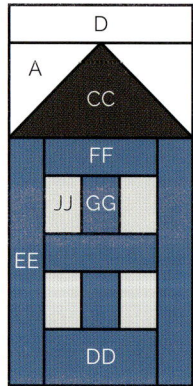

Make eight.
You will not use all Fabric CC rectangles.

Tree Blocks:

Each Tree Block uses two coordinating prints.

Draw a diagonal line on the wrong side of the Fabric K squares.

With right sides facing, layer Fabric K squares on opposite corners of a Fabric LL rectangle.

Stitch on the drawn lines and trim ¼" away from the seams.

Repeat on the remaining corners.

Short Tree Top Unit should measure 2 ½" x 7 ½".

Make six.

Assemble Block using coordinating fabric.

Short Tree Block should measure 2 ½" x 10 ½".

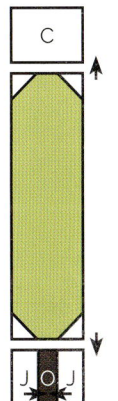 

Make six.

With right sides facing, layer Fabric K squares on opposite corners of a Fabric KK rectangle.

Stitch on the drawn lines and trim ¼" away from the seams.

Repeat on the remaining corners.

Tall Tree Top Unit should measure 2 ¾" x 8 ½".

Make six.

Assemble Block using coordinating fabric.

Tall Tree Block should measure 2 ¾" x 10 ½".

Make six.

Carrie's Neighborhood Quilt

Quilt Center:

Assemble Quilt Center. Press toward the sashing.

Quilt Center should measure 54 ½" x 58 ½".

Border:

Attach side borders using the Fabric L1 strips.

Attach top and bottom borders using the Fabric L2 strips.

Finishing:

Piece the Fabric MM strips end to end for binding.

Quilt and bind as desired.

Joanna's Neighborhood Quilt

Joanna's version of the Neighborhood Quilt has a different fabric in the borders!

Designed by: Joanna Figueroa / Sewn by: Joanna Figueroa and Friends
Quilted by: Diana Johnson (Instagram: @quiltedgrammy)

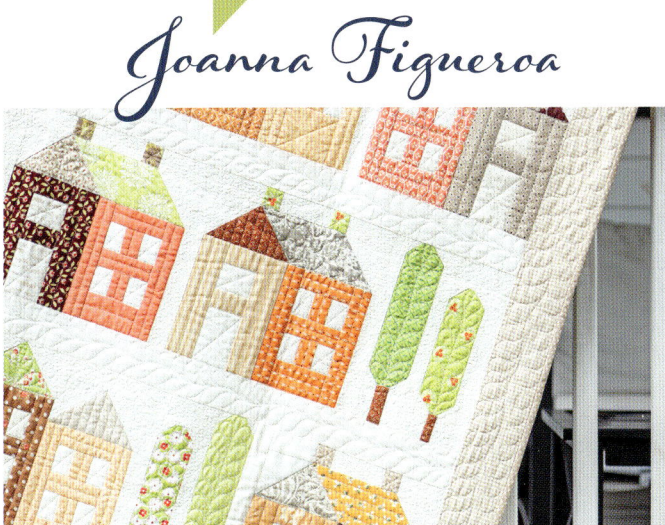

"As soon as I saw this Neighborhood Quilt, I knew that I wanted a few of my quilt "village" friends to help me work on it. So each of us, Cynthia, Diana, Susan, Cheryl and myself, worked on one row then sent it off to Diana to join together and do her quilting magic. It was really so much fun building our neighborhood together. Wouldn't it be wonderful to do the same thing for a Christmas neighborhood or a patriotic summer one?"

Joanna Figueroa

Neighborhood Tablerunner

18 ½" x 51 ½"

Designed by: Joanna Figueroa / Sewn by: Kimberly Jolly (Instagram: @fatquartershop)
Quilted by: Gina Tell (Instagram: @gina_tell_threadgraffiti)

Fabric Requirements:

½ yard - Background and Inner Border

1 - 3" x WOF strip, subcut into:	
10 - 3" squares	A
from the remainder of strip cut:	
2 - 2" x 2 ½" rectangles	B
3 - 1 ½" x WOF strips, subcut into:	
4 - 1 ½" x 10 ½" rectangles	C
2 - 1 ½" x 10 ½" strips	D
1 - 1 ½" x 5 ½" rectangle	E
2 - 1 ½" x 3 ½" rectangles	F
4 - 1 ½" x 3" rectangles	G
from the remainder of strip cut:	
4 - 1 ¼" x 2" rectangles	H
8 - 1 ¼" squares	I
3 - 1 ½" x WOF strips, sew end to end and subcut into:	
2 - 1 ½" x 45 ½" strips	J

1 Layer Cake square - House Roof Side, Chimneys and Tree Trunk

From the 10" square cut:	
2 - 3" x 8" rectangles	K
4 - 1 ½" squares	L
2 - 1" x 2" rectangles	M

2 Layer Cake squares - House Roof Front

From each 10" square cut:	
1 - 3" x 5 ½" rectangle (2 total)	N

2 Layer Cake squares - House Front

From each 10" square cut:	
2 - 2" x 7" rectangles (4 total)	O
2 - 1 ½" x 2 ½" rectangles (4 total)	P

2 Layer Cake squares - House Side

From each 10" square cut:	
1 - 2" x 3 ½" rectangle (2 total)	Q
2 - 1 ½" x 7" rectangles (4 total)	R
2 - 1 ½" x 3 ½" rectangles (4 total)	S
2 - 1 ½" x 2" rectangles (4 total)	T

2 Layer Cake squares - House Door and Windows

From each 10" square cut:	
1 - 2 ½" x 3 ½" rectangle (2 total)	U
1 - 2" x 2 ½" rectangle (2 total)	V
4 - 1 ½" x 2" rectangles (8 total)	W

3 Layer Cake squares - Condo Roof

From each 10" square cut:	
1 - 3" x 5 ½" rectangle (3 total)	X

2 Layer Cake squares - Tall Condo Front

From each 10" square cut:	
1 - 3" x 3 ½" rectangle (2 total)	Y
2 - 1 ½" x 8" rectangles (4 total)	Z
2 - 1 ½" x 3 ½" rectangles (4 total)	AA
2 - 1 ½" x 2" rectangles (4 total)	BB

1 Layer Cake square - Short Condo Front

From the 10" square cut:	
1 - 2" x 3 ½" rectangle	CC
2 - 1 ½" x 7" rectangles	DD
2 - 1 ½" x 3 ½" rectangles	EE
2 - 1 ½" x 2" rectangles	FF

3 Layer Cake squares - Condo Windows

From each 10" square cut:	
4 - 1 ½" x 2" rectangles (12 total)	GG

1 Layer Cake square - Tree Top

From the 10" square cut:	
2 - 2 ½" x 7 ½" rectangles	HH

⅝ yard - Outer Border

4 - 3 ½" x WOF strips, sew end to end and subcut into:	
2 - 3 ½" x 12 ½" strips	II
2 - 3 ½" x 51 ½" strips	JJ

½ yard - Binding

5 - 2 ¼" x WOF strips	KK

1 ¾ yards - Backing

Neighborhood Tablerunner

House Blocks:

Refer to pages 146 to 151 for House Block instructions.

Each House Block uses five coordinating prints.

Assemble Block using coordinating fabric.
Left House Block should measure 10 ½" x 10 ½".

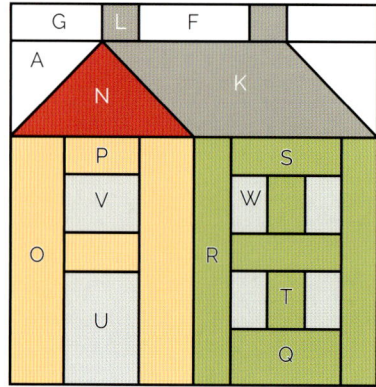

Make one.

Assemble Block using coordinating fabric.
Right House Block should measure 10 ½" x 10 ½".

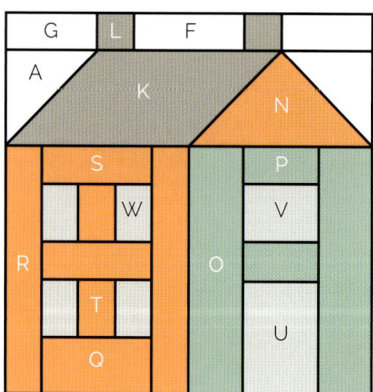

Make one.

Condo Blocks:

Refer to pages 152 to 153 for Condo Block instructions.

Each Condo Block uses three coordinating prints.

Assemble Block using coordinating fabric.
Tall Condo Block should measure 5 ½" x 10 ½".

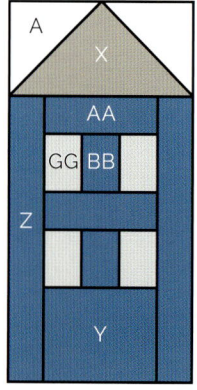

Make two.

Assemble Block using coordinating fabric.
Short Condo Block should measure 5 ½" x 10 ½".

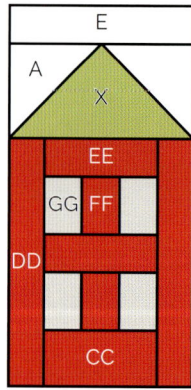

Make one.

Meet Kimberly Jolly

Kimberly, Joanna and Carrie started off on this crazy quilt adventure at about the same time, business owners trying to figure out how to make this all work. Joanna and Kimberly became fast friends, sharing adventures along the way, whether sewing in a hotel room in Waco or sharing an impromptu weekend in Hollywood with their husbands, looking for movie stars! Carrie got to know Kimberly through work, patterns and business, leading to them working together on books and videos. Now if they could just agree on washing quilts!

Off the Cuff ...

PULLING FABRIC FOR A SCRAP QUILT

« Carrie »

When I'm pulling fabric for a scrap quilt, there are several things I like to do.

Arranging: After I have a selection of fabrics and colors, I lay them out randomly. Meaning, they are not arranged by color or value, they are purposely mixed. Then I mix them up again. That lets me see if there are fabrics that stand out or disappear. It also lets me get a feel for the mood of the palette.

Zingers: If there is a fabric that really stands out, I don't take it out. I add more of that color! I like scrap quilts that have a little bit of clash … some zing.

Scale: I love how big prints look when they're cut up into little pieces. Some of the pieces are mushy, while others are choppy. They have movement and energy, and I like that.

Cuttings: The key here is to start with a clean basket or bin for cuttings (a.k.a. the bits that will be thrown away). Since I like to cut most of the quilt before I start piecing, I use the trash-pieces to get a sense of how the fabrics will look in the finished quilt. As I'm adding to the bin, I mix it up to see how it looks. Do the fabrics all blend together? Is it creating a mood or a feel? Are there one or two fabrics that stand out, no matter what?

« Joanna »

Scrap quilts are at the very top of my list of favorite quilts to make. To be honest, I don't get to make them as often as I would like, since the life of a pattern and fabric designer forces me to design quilts that go with a specific collection or palette. So when I get a chance to go scrappy, I take it. And hence the quilts in this book … all scrappilicious! While I have no method of pulling the fabric for a scrap quilt, I intuitively vary scale, color and style of fabric until I have my palette. I almost always have to put fabrics back because I have chosen too many and I have to edit. Once I start making the quilt, I start to pay attention to what goes where. Is each block balanced? Is each row more or less even in tone and scale? At that point, I always determine the strongest colors in the group. My very scientific method for doing that? I take my glasses off and squint. Once I determine which fabrics are the strong ones, I make sure they are balanced throughout the blocks, rows and overall design. The colors that most often fall into that category? Black and charcoal, of course. But also red, darker aqua, plum and darker browns. Most of the other colors in the "Fig Tree rainbow" will all play very nicely together.

Scrap bins and cuttings? I don't even look at them these days. That is definitely one thing that has changed over the years. I used to save all of those scrap triangles, but I know myself well enough to know that I will never go back, so nowadays I just let them go.

Neighborhood Tablerunner

Draw a diagonal line on the wrong side of the Fabric I squares.

With right sides facing, layer Fabric I squares on opposite corners of a Fabric HH rectangle.

Stitch on the drawn lines and trim ¼" away from the seams.

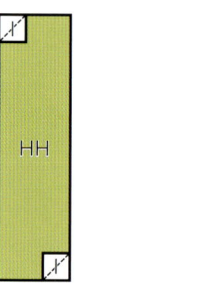 

Repeat on the remaining corners.
Tree Top Unit should measure 2 ½" x 7 ½".

Make two.

Assemble Block.
Tree Block should measure 2 ½" x 10 ½".

Make two.

Tablerunner Center:

Assemble Tablerunner Center.

Tablerunner Center should measure 10 ½" x 43 ½".

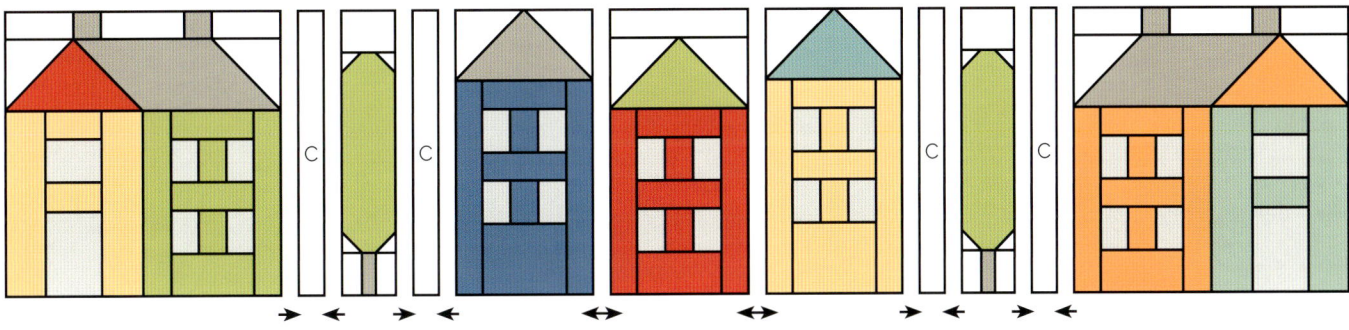

Border:

Attach side inner borders using the Fabric D strips. Attach top and bottom inner borders using the Fabric J strips.

Attach side outer borders using the Fabric II strips. Attach top and bottom outer borders using the Fabric JJ strips.

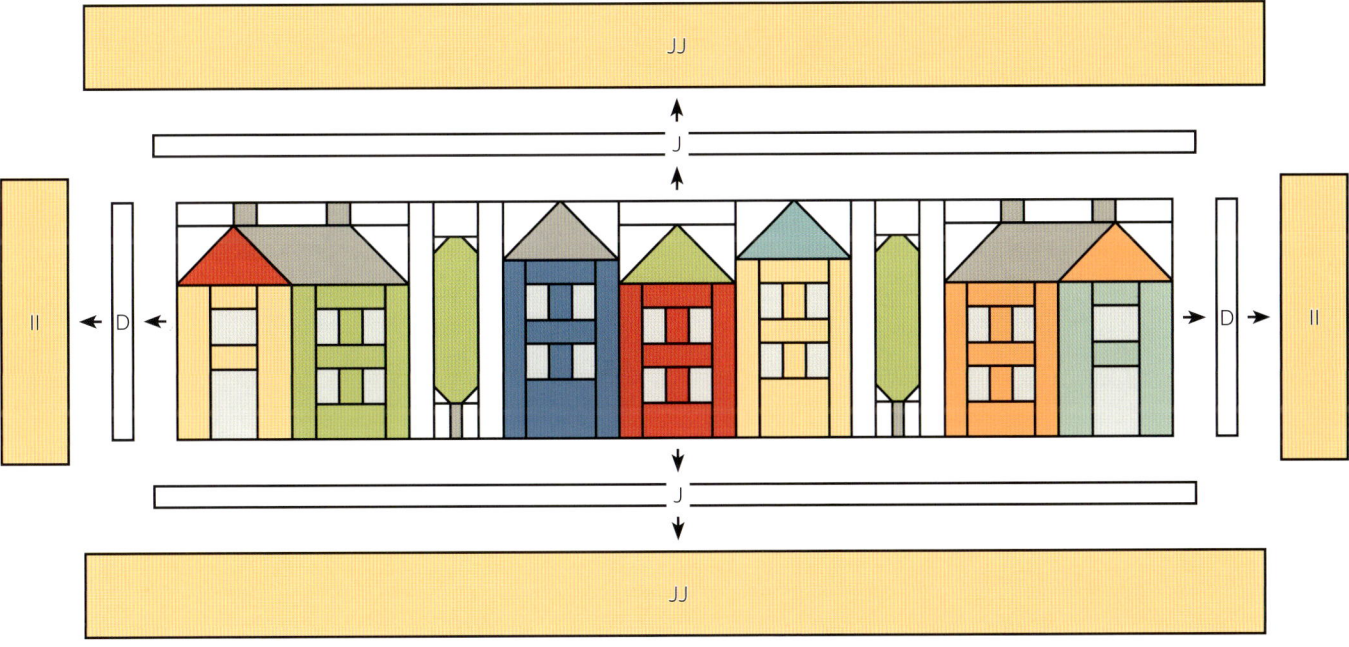

Finishing:

Piece the Fabric KK strips end to end for binding.

Quilt and bind as desired.

Joanna's Neighborhood Pillow

25" x 25"

Designed, Sewn and Quilted by: Joanna Figueroa

Fabric Requirements:

⅓ yard - Background

1 - 3" x WOF strip, subcut into: 8 - 3" squares	A
1 - 1 ½" x WOF strip, subcut into: 4 - 1 ½" x 3 ½" rectangles	B
8 - 1 ½" x 3" rectangles	C

4 Charm Pack squares - Chimneys

From each 5" square cut: 2 - 1 ½" squares (8 total)	D

4 Layer Cake squares - House Front

From each 10" square cut: 2 - 2" x 7" rectangles (8 total)	E
2 - 1 ½" x 2 ½" rectangles (8 total)	F

4 Layer Cake squares - House Side

From each 10" square cut: 1 - 2" x 3 ½" rectangle (4 total)	G
2 - 1 ½" x 7" rectangles (8 total)	H
2 - 1 ½" x 3 ½" rectangles (8 total)	I
2 - 1 ½" x 2" rectangles (8 total)	J

4 Layer Cake squares - Roof Front

From each 10" square cut: 1 - 3" x 5 ½" rectangle (4 total)	K

4 Layer Cake squares - Roof Side

From each 10" square cut: 1 - 3" x 8" rectangle (4 total)	L

4 Layer Cake squares - Door and Front Window

From each 10" square cut: 1 - 2 ½" x 3 ½" rectangle (4 total)	M
1 - 2" x 2 ½" rectangle (4 total)	N

We have pillow finishing instructions and tips on page 14!

4 Layer Cake squares - Side Windows	
From each 10" square cut: 4 - 1 ½" x 2" rectangles (16 total)	O
1 Fat Eighth - Sashing	
From the 9" x 21" rectangle cut: 4 - 1 ½" x 10 ½" rectangles	P
1 Charm Pack square - Cornerstone	
From the 5" square cut: 1 - 1 ½" square	Q
½ yard - Border	
4 - 2 ½" x WOF strips, subcut into: 2 - 2 ½" x 25 ½" strips 2 - 2 ½" x 21 ½" strips	R S

Left House Blocks:

Refer to pages 146 to 148 for Left House Block instructions.

Each House Block uses seven coordinating prints.

Assemble Block using coordinating fabric.
Left House Block should measure 10 ½" x 10 ½".

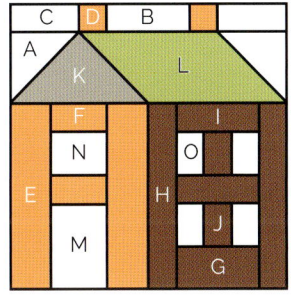

Make four total.

Pillow Center:

Assemble Pillow Center. Press toward the sashing.
Pillow Center should measure 21 ½" x 21 ½".

Border:

Attach side borders using the Fabric S strips.

Attach top and bottom borders using the Fabric R strips.

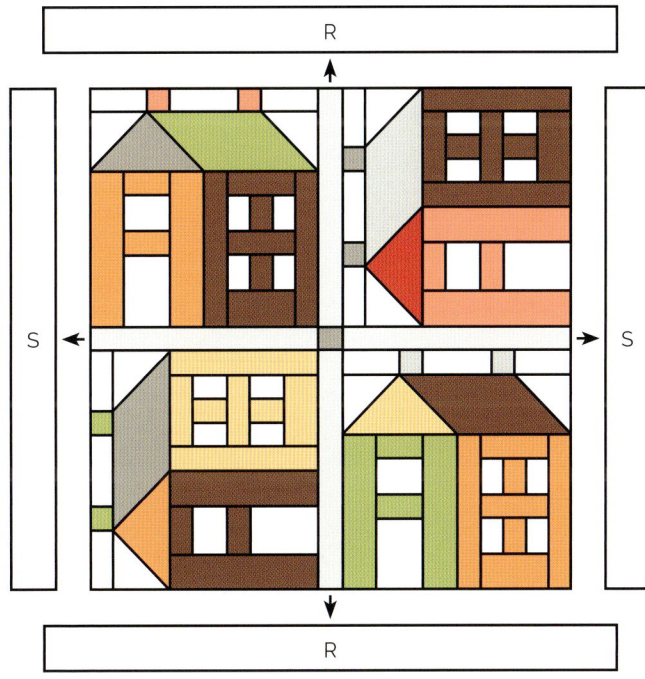

Carrie's Neighborhood Pillow

25" x 25"

Designed, Sewn and Quilted by: Carrie Nelson

Fabric Requirements:

⅓ yard - Background	
1 - 3" x WOF strip, subcut into:	
8 - 3" squares	A
1 - 1 ½" x WOF strip, subcut into:	
4 - 1 ½" x 3 ½" rectangles	B
8 - 1 ½" x 3" rectangles	C

1 Layer Cake square - Chimneys	
From the 10" square cut:	
8 - 1 ½" squares	D

4 Layer Cake squares - House Front	
From each 10" square cut:	
2 - 2" x 7" rectangles (8 total)	E
2 - 1 ½" x 2 ½" rectangles (8 total)	F

4 Layer Cake squares - House Side	
From each 10" square cut:	
1 - 2" x 3 ½" rectangle (4 total)	G
2 - 1 ½" x 7" rectangles (8 total)	H
2 - 1 ½" x 3 ½" rectangles (8 total)	I
2 - 1 ½" x 2" rectangles (8 total)	J

4 Layer Cake squares - Roof Front	
From each 10" square cut:	
1 - 3" x 5 ½" rectangle (4 total)	K

4 Layer Cake squares - Roof Side	
From each 10" square cut:	
1 - 3" x 8" rectangle (4 total)	L

4 Layer Cake squares - Windows	
From each 10" square cut:	
1 - 2" x 2 ½" rectangle (4 total)	M
4 - 1 ½" x 2" rectangles (16 total)	N

We have pillow finishing instructions and tips on page 14!

4 Charm Pack squares - Door	
From each 5" square cut: 1 - 2 ½" x 3 ½" rectangle (4 total)	O
¼ yard - Sashing	
2 - 1 ½" x WOF strips, subcut into: 1 - 1 ½" x 21 ½" strip 2 - 1 ½" x 10 ½" rectangles	P Q
½ yard - Border	
4 - 2 ½" x WOF strips, subcut into: 2 - 2 ½" x 25 ½" strips 2 - 2 ½" x 21 ½" strips	R S

Left House Blocks:

Refer to pages 146 to 148 for Left House Block instructions.

Each House Block uses seven coordinating prints.

Assemble Block using coordinating fabric.
Left House Block should measure 10 ½" x 10 ½".

Make four total.

Pillow Center:

Assemble Pillow Center. Press toward the sashing.
Pillow Center should measure 21 ½" x 21 ½".

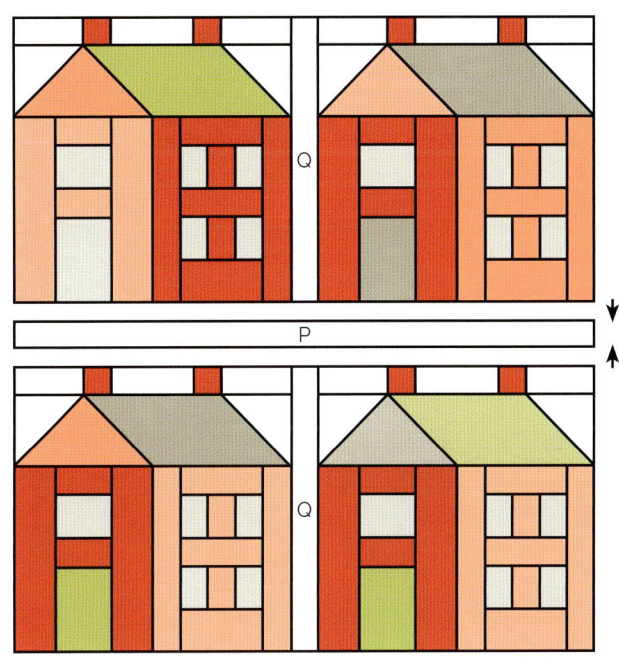

Border:

Attach side borders using the Fabric S strips.
Attach top and bottom borders using the Fabric R strips.

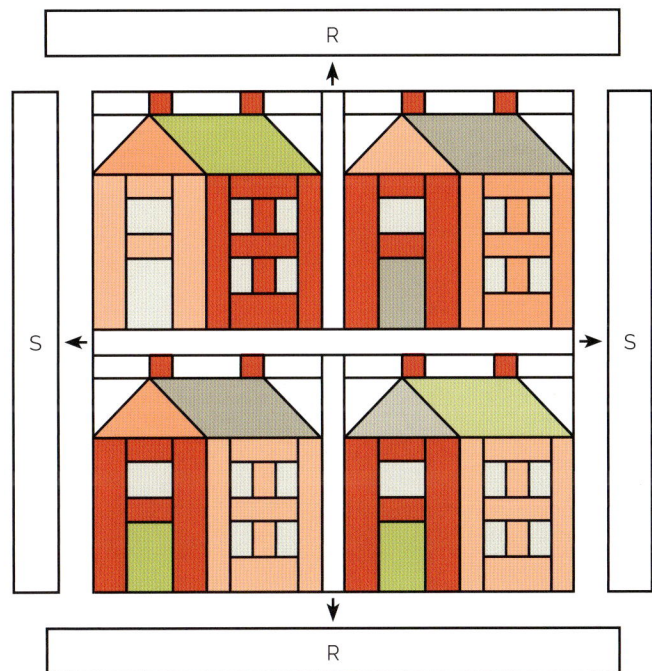

Neighborhood Condo Pillow

16" x 20"

Fabric Requirements:

Designed, Sewn and Quilted by: Carrie Nelson

½ yard - Background and Border	
1 - 3" x WOF strip, subcut into: 6 - 3" squares	A
from the remainder of strip cut: 12 - 1 ½" x 2" rectangles	B
1 - 1 ¼" x WOF strip, subcut into: 2 - 1 ¼" x 10 ½" rectangles	C
1 - 3 ½" x WOF strip, subcut into: 2 - 3 ½" x 21" strips	D
1 - 2 ½" x WOF strip, subcut into: 2 - 2 ½" x 11" strips	E

3 Layer Cake squares - Condo Roof	
From each 10" square cut: 1 - 3" x 5 ½" rectangle (3 total)	F

3 Layer Cake squares - Tall Condo Front	
From each 10" square cut: 1 - 3" x 3 ½" rectangle (3 total)	G
2 - 1 ½" x 8" rectangles (6 total)	H
2 - 1 ½" x 3 ½" rectangles (6 total)	I
2 - 1 ½" x 2" rectangles (6 total)	J

1 Fat Eighth - Grass	
From the 9" x 21" rectangle cut: 1 - 1" x 17" rectangle	K

We have pillow finishing instructions and tips on page 14!